D1032825

ACKNOWLEDGMENTS

The author and The Free Press acknowledge, with thanks, the permission granted by publishers and copyright holders to reprint papers included in this volume. The place of original publication of each of the chapters is listed below.

1. "The Scope and History of Theories of Economic Growth" was first published in Revista de Economia Politica, Vol. 5, No. 1 (May, 1953), pp. 9-28.

2. "Social Structure and Economic Growth" was first published in Economia Internazionale, Vol. 6, No. 3 (August, 1953), pp. 52-77.

3. "A Sociological Approach to Economic Development" was first published in Atti del Congresso Internazionale di Studio sul Problema delle Aree Arretrate, II, 755-78, Milan: Centro Nazionale di Prevenzione e Difesa Sociale, 1955.

4. "Patterns of Economic Growth" was first published in The Canadian Journal of Economics and Political Science, Vol. 21, No. 4 (November, 1955), pp. 416-31.

5. "Population Pressure, Industrialization, and Social Mobility" was first published in Population Studies, Vol. II, No. 2 (November, 1957), pp. 123-35.

6. "Entrepreneurship and Economic Growth" was first published in The American Journal of Economics and Sociology, Vol. 12, No. 1 (October, 1952), pp. 97-110.

7. "The Role of Cities in the Economic Growth of Underdeveloped Countries" was first published in The Journal of Political Economy, Vol. 61, No. 3 (June, 1953) pp. 195-208.

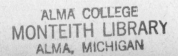

8. "Generative and Parasitic Cities" was first published in
Economic Development and Cultural Change, Vol. 3, No. 3
(April, 1955), pp. 278-94.

9. "Urbanization and Economic Growth in Asia" was first published in Economic Development and Cultural Change, Vol. 6, No. 1
(October, 1957), pp. 42-54.

CONTENTS

1

INTRODUCTION: THE SCOPE AND HISTORY OF THEORIES OF ECONOMIC GROWTH

Of all branches of economics none has made such rapid gain in popularity during the postwar period as the analysis of long-run economic growth. In the United States there has appeared a flood of journal articles on various aspects of economic growth which was supplemented by several books purporting to present a new theory of long-run economic development. In several colleges and universities this area was designated as a new field of specialization for graduate students in economics. Textbooks have not been lacking and there is reason to believe that more publications of different types will continue to appear in considerable quantity for some time to come.

Against the claim that this field constitutes an entirely new interest of economists, the argument has been raised that long-run economic problems have always been a concern of economists, and that, moreover, these questions are not unique but merely require the application of the principles of short-run analysis to phenomena occurring over a somewhat longer period. In support of this it was further argued that the theory of business cycles can be applied with few modifications to problems of growth. Growth theorists have, in turn, replied that they are concerned with "secular" problems and that short-run analysis and cyclical analysis is only of limited usefulness. Some of them have maintained that a new economic theory of long-run growth needs to be developed, whereas others have held that the most important aspects of such a theory would be the inclusion of political and sociological factors rather than a new statement of purely economic relations.

I

Instead of taking sides in this dispute I wish to touch upon two points which underlie these contrasting views. First I wish to express the opinion that the question of whether or not the presently available tools of economics are suited for the analysis of long-run economic growth can be judged best after a consideration of the standard economic literature explicitly concerned with underdeveloped countries. Some of the most meritorious contributions to this literature deal with such typical economic problems, as capital formation, the development of an industrial labor force, monetary and fiscal aspects of economic development, the impact of economic growth on living standards and consumption levels, and the problems of balance of payment difficulties, as well as the need for and difficulties of developmental planning. Though a large part of the analysis is built on a foundation firmly anchored in economic theory as commonly accepted, a somewhat different emphasis is placed on several variables from that which is customary in general economic theory or the analysis of economic problems of advanced countries. One example is the explicit emphasis placed upon leisure as a form of income as against monetary income; another is the concern with the interpersonal distribution of increments of national income; a third is the strong orientation towards treating theoretical questions from a viewpoint of effective economic policy. In part these instances of altered emphasis are due to the practical problems faced by developing countries, especially those which have extensive and detailed development plans. But in part it is a recognition that western economic analysis is being applied to cultures in which some of the values that are taken for granted in occidental countries are either completely absent or are present only in strongly modified forms, and that, therefore, certain forms of economic behavior which commonly occur in western countries often cannot be found in developing economies with the same regularity and frequency. In principle, many of these differences in the two types of society can probably be handled by applying the theory of monopoly or discrimination, or the concept of non-competing groups. But these parts of traditional economic analysis have not been absorbed as yet in a fully satisfactory manner into theories of economic growth or theories explaining the economic growth or theories explaining the economic problems of developing countries.

Other concepts which are familiar in traditional economic theory but which take on much greater importance in the theoretical analysis of the economics of developing countries are those of bottlenecks of supply and of economies or diseconomies external to an industry. Modern economists are, of course, familiar with these concepts and their practical occurrence. But in most instances bottlenecks of supply, as well as external diseconomies are assumed to be short-run phenomena which may normally be eliminated in a limited period of time. In underdeveloped countries bottlenecks of supply may be of considerable duration and there may be a few and, in extreme cases, no alternatives to get around them. Capital rationing, especially for certain types of investment, the lack of certain types of labor, especially certain

types of skilled labor, are instances of this kind which have occurred at crucial junctures in many underdeveloped countries.
Similarly the absence of many external economies has become
one of the chief explanatory factors for instances of chronic
underdevelopment in some regions of the world. Any theory
which purports to deal adequately with the economic problems
of underdeveloped countries would have to pay explicit and extended attention to the solution of problems created by the appearance of chronic bottlenecks of supply and the lasting absence of
economies external to the industry in various fields of production.

II

The second major problem which I wish to discuss briefly is
the question of whether we are justified in assuming that theories
of economic growth, such as they exist, are the product of the
last few years or whether they have already been formulated earlier. This question is important, since the existence of earlier
theories may broaden our own viewpoint if we review them critically. It is too well known to require special demonstration that
economic theories have been developed in the past in response to
practical problems in the social and economic field which required
a solution. For example, the great depressions of the 1870's and
the 1930's stimulated theoretical work in monetary analysis and
the theory of employment and resulted in a modern theory of banking and credit and Keynesian economics. Similarly, the most
important "external" incentive for the current interest on the part
of economists in a theory of long-run economic growth are the
vigorous efforts made by the countries of Asia, Africa, and Latin
America to raise the productivity and levels of output of their

economies. But if we witness today conscious efforts to stimulate economic growth in the so-called underdeveloped countries of the world, we should not forget that the advanced countries were, at an earlier period, undergoing their own initial phases of growth, and we should expect that the economic literature of these periods would reflect also this aspect of economic reality.

There are, above all, three periods in the earlier history of economic thought when the conditions and probably the outcomes of secular economic growth were discussed at some length. The first is the period of early industrialization in Europe which coincides in time with what is commonly referred to as the period of mercantilist economics. The second is the period of the Industrial Revolution in England, the years from about 1775 to 1832. This period coincides with the elaboration of classical economics, especially the first statement of the Malthusian and Ricardian system of economic theory. The third period falls in the third quarter of the nineteenth century when other countries, notably Germany and the United States, began to catch up with Britain, and finally overtook it as the leading industrial power in the world. This period coincides with the development of a body of economic thought in Germany which in its theoretical content is considerably inferior to classical economics, but which, as we shall see, has given more explicit attention to problems of secular growth than did the classical economists.

III

It is not necessary, in this place, to solve the question of whether the economic writings of the seventeenth and eighteenth centuries form a system or not. The mercantilists have many ideas

in common, and yet there are considerable differences among
different writers, the main themes discussed at different periods,
and the foci of interest in different countries. In fact, differences in the mercantilist literature elaborated in various countries have been sufficiently impressive to lead one careful stu-
dent of that literature to distinguish between German, French,
and British mercantilism in attributing to the first a population-
ist, to the second an industrialist, and to the third a commercial-
ist bias (1). Since almost all mercantilist writings had the objective of proposing policies which would lead to the strengthening
of the state, this classification points to the main variable which
in each country was seen to occupy the central position. Whatever may be the characteristics which distinguish the writings of
European economic writers of the period 1550 to 1750 from the
earlier and later economic literature, demographic questions,
the fostering of industry, and the regulation of commerce play an
important role in the economic thought of all of them, though var-
iously emphasized in different countries. Since the mercantilist
writers developed a crude labor theory of value and considered
the total social product to be directly correlated with the size of
the labor force, an increase of population was clearly a means of
increasing the annual gross product of a country and hence the
power of the state. Similarly, in a society in which improvements in agriculture were slow and halting and in which there
existed, therefore, a tendency towards low marginal productivity
in farming, the artificial stimulation of industry, either by direct
or indirect government subsidization or by inflationary pressure,

was a means to the same end. In France, chief emphasis was placed upon subsidization of industry; in England, where independent entrepreneurship was more abundant, major emphasis was placed upon creating a climate which would favor the growth of manufactures and commerce. The latter, especially foreign trade, was seen as an indispensable adjunct of improving manufactures since it provided a country lacking many raw materials with the necessary resources through importation, and permitted the disposal of the products of manufacture. Unlike Holland, where the hegemony of trade had led to institutions which allowed indigenous manufactures and even agriculture to stagnate, the traders in Britain never attained so dominating a position as to enable them to disregard the claims of a growing industry. Industrial development in England was aided by the supply of a cheap labor force, which became available through the enclosure movement which reached its peak in the eighteenth century. It was aided also by "profit inflation." To this end the mercantilist writers advocated policies designed to produce an export surplus, low interest rates, and, in the last resort, an artificial increase in the quantity of money through credit expansion and the creation of paper money. The balance of trade doctrine of Thomas Mun, the suggestion for governmental lowering of interest rates by Josiah Child, and the theories of monetary and credit expansion of John Law are stages in an economic policy designed to increase the circulating medium in a country and to provide thereby the conditions of profit inflation and industrial expansion. A somewhat simplified model of the "mercantilist" theory of economic growth stated in present-day terminology, would present the following aspects: Gross national product is a function of the size of the labor force, and quantity of capital, and the quantity of money (or money substitutes). The last two variables, capital and the quantity of money, are not independent, since the quantity of capital, in turn, is a function of the quantity of money and of governmental policies designed to create or at least encourage real investment.

This model shows clearly that the mercantilists did not confuse money and wealth. It does support, however, the view, which was quite generally held by mercantilist writers in all countries, that the quantity of money was one of the preconditions of wealth, i. e. , of gross social output. This model may appear very simple-minded and almost obvious. Its simpleness is partly due to the fact that the attempt is here made to sketch the most general set of variables common to all or almost all writers of the mercantilist period. If we were to discuss in more detail the views of any one particular writer, we would doubtless arrive at a somewhat more complex model. We cannot enter into such detailed investigation in this place, but there is no doubt that, in view of the many similarities between the economic problems facing a number of European countries and territories in mercantilist times and those facing several underdeveloped countries today, a closer examination of mercantilist literature might prove a very useful undertaking. In making such a comparison we must not forget that one of the greatest shortcomings of mercantilist

views on economic growth was the absence of any realistic economic theory of investment. For most of them the creation of capital was so closely bound up with political decisions that they looked
at investment essentially as a political act. On the other hand,
they were quite realistic in their interpretation of the role of the
human factor in development, especially in pointing repeatedly
to the need of considering the creation of "human capital, " a
matter which must often be consciously planned. Many proposals
for the "useful employment" of the "labouring poor" and their
children imply such a view and, unlike the later economic literature in which the acquisition of higher skills by a person was
considered essentially to be a matter of private cost, they saw
that the recruitment and training of a qualified industrial labor
force should properly be regarded as involving a large element
of social cost. Many such conceptions as this were underplayed
or entirely forgotten as a consequence of the destruction of mercantilist theories by Adam Smith and his followers. The decisive
victory of extreme liberalism, according to which each person
was master of his own fate, and which considered not merely programs of public assistance, but, in extreme cases, even programs
of public education, as illegitimate interferences with the freedom
of the market, robbed the views of mercantilists of their res-
pectability. One of the concomitant changes was the replacement
of a theory in which population growth was looked upon with favor
as a stimulus to economic growth by one in which population growth
became the "diabolus" ex machina which tended to lead an ultimate
state of economic stagnation.

IV

This change introduces the classical theory of economic growth and the main pillar on which it was built, the Malthusian theory of population. In stipulating differential growth rates of population and total product, Malthus was extrapolating a long-run trend of economic development. Though his ultimate expectations were pessimistic and presaged stagnation rather than growth, his original theory, nevertheless, must be regarded as an attempt not merely to indicate the expected outcome of the process of secular change, but also to identify the variables determining the outcome.

Malthus' views on secular development were taken over by Ricardo. But Ricardo was primarily interested in analyzing the distribution of the social product among recipients of wages, profit, and rent, rather than in modifying the secular theories of Malthus. Malthus' contribution to the theory of secular economic change lay, therefore, in pointing out the impact of population growth on the one hand, and the consequences of the limitation of one factor (land), on the other. Ricardo's main contribution was his attempt to determine the relative shares which the owners of each factor received and the conditions which would change these relative shares over time. The combined theory may be outlined in the form of a simple model which was recently presented by T. Haavelmo, whose discussion we will follow (2).

Though neither Malthus nor Ricardo had a clear concept of a production function, such as was developed on the basis of the work of Marshall and his contemporaries of the neoclassical school, we will, nevertheless, use this device in order to present the basic feature of the Malthus-Ricardo model. If we designate the two factors of production, labor and capital, by L and K, and if we designate the total output by Y, we can set up a social production function of the Cobb-Douglas type of the following form:

$$Y = bL^{\alpha} K^{\beta} \qquad (1)$$

where α and β are positive parameters, but the sum of $\alpha + \beta$ is less than unity, because of the assumption of decreasing returns. This assumption simply means that in the long run alterations in scale are not linear because there is at least one factor of production, viz., land, which presents a chronic supply bottleneck.

Now let us further suppose that Y is divided into two shares, that of laborers which is all consumed and that of capitalists and landowners which is accumulated, apart from a relatively small portion which is consumed by them. Finally let us suppose that the rate of wages, w, is determined by the marginal productivity of labor so that

Profits, g, is then:
$$w = \frac{\partial Y}{\partial L} = b\alpha L^{\alpha-1} K^{\beta} . \qquad (2)$$
$$g = Y - wL = (1-\alpha) Y . \qquad (3)$$

If we assume for the sake of simplicity that all profits are reinvested we obtain for investment, I, the formula:

$$I = g = (1-\alpha) Y . \qquad (4)$$

Since α and Y are positive and $0 < \alpha < 1$, the amount of investment is a positive fraction of total product and depends in its magnitude on the magnitude of Y.

So far we have presented an approximate description of the Ricardian view of the distribution of the social product between wage workers and property owners. Now the Malthusian part of the theory, that dealing with the problem of population, is superimposed. Suppose, Malthus would say, that as long as the wage level is above a certain (physiologically determined) minimum, w_o , population tends to grow very rapidly. Since the actual wage, w, never rises very substantially above w_o , any short-run increase of the wage is sufficient to provoke a large enough upsurge of population to bring the wage down to the minimum wage. In fact, Malthus would say, there is a tendency for the poor to increase their number even when this wage is reached, so that various checks will come into play in order to reduce the population to a level where the wage, w_o , can be maintained. However, as the total amount of K increases, more and more persons are enabled to live at the subsistence level, w_o . In other words, if, once the whole world is inhabited, population would increase in an arithmetic ratio as resources do, and would not show tendencies to increase in a geometric ratio, then there would be progress; but this progress would consist in a proportional increase in the total quantity of capital and the total number of workers. There would be no increase in the standard of living since, by hypothesis, every increase in living standards, i.e., wages, would lead to a sufficient increment of population to wipe out again the increased standard of living.

But although progress consists in an increase of capital, and hence in an increase of the total mass of profit, the rate of profit will fall. From equation (2) we find that $L = \dfrac{\alpha Y}{w_o}$,

so that $Y = b L^{\alpha} K^{\beta} = b \left(\dfrac{\alpha Y}{w_o} \right)^{\alpha} K^{\beta} = \left[b \left(\dfrac{\alpha}{w_o} \right)^{\alpha} K^{\beta} \right]^{\frac{1}{1-\alpha}}$.

From this we derive the rate of profit, π,

$$\pi = \frac{g}{K} = \frac{(1-\alpha)Y}{K} = (1-\alpha) \left[b \left(\frac{\alpha}{w_o} \right)^{\alpha} \right]^{\frac{1}{1-\alpha}} K^{\frac{\beta}{1-\alpha} - 1} . \qquad (5)$$

Since $(1-\alpha)\left[b\left(\dfrac{\alpha}{w_0}\right)^{\alpha}\right]^{\frac{1}{1-\alpha}}$ is a constant, the rate of profit, π, depends upon $K^{\frac{\beta}{1-\alpha}-1}$. But if $0 < \alpha < 1$ and $0 < \beta < 1$, the value of π will decrease with increasing K.

The tendency of the rate of profit to fall was thought to be a cause of the gradual reduction and eventual stagnation of capital accumulation. It should be noted that the theory is based upon the assumption of diminishing returns. For if they are assumed away, the sum of $\alpha + \beta$ needs not be smaller than one, and then we could have, in an extreme case, even an increasing rate of profit with an increasing quantity of capital. We can see, moreover, that under the assumption that total profits are reinvested, we obtain a faster growth of the value of K than if we assume that part of it is spent on consumption. Malthus knew this also and hence he favored luxury expenditures by the rich and the aristocracy, particularly because the increasing pressure of population on land (the factor in limited supply) would have the consequence of secularly increasing rents.

At the same time, we can see what could be expected if Malthus' advice was followed and moral or prudential restraint was successfully practiced. In this case, the level of wages could increase as the growth of capital gradually causes the marginal productivity of a constant quantity of labor to increase. Assume, for example, that the total labor force were kept constant at the level L_o. In this case, w would increase with an increasing K according to a relationship derivable from equation (2):

$$w = b \, \alpha \, L_o^{\alpha-1} \, K^{\beta} \, , \tag{6}$$

whereas the rate of profits would still fall, according to the formula, derived from equations (4) and (5):

$$\pi = \frac{(1-\alpha)Y}{K} = (1-\alpha)\, b \, L_o^{\alpha} K^{\beta-1} \, . \tag{7}$$

Thus, if population remains stable or increases at a slower rate than the quantity of capital, wages may rise, even though the principle of diminishing returns operates. In this instance, however, the rate of profit falls, as before, and, given the assumptions of the classical economists, leads eventually to a stoppage in the accumulation of capital. The crucial problem which a society faced was how to overcome the law of the falling rate of profit, and it is clear that the only manner in which this could be achieved was by eliminating the principle of decreasing returns, and replacing it by a principle of constant or increasing returns. This was one of the tentatively offered solutions of the neoclassical school, and virtually the only comment made by Alfred Marshall on the problem of long-run economic growth is his discussion of the counterbalancing effects of diminishing and increasing returns (3).

But Marshall had, in a sense, already been anticipated by William Godwin against whose original theories Malthus's book on population was directed. In his effort to reply to the strictures of Malthus, Godwin produced, in 1820, a book which contains his full and final rebuttal. It is a meandering, wordy, cantankerous book. But it contains one delightful passage which Godwin's contemporaries must have regarded as pure phantasy, but which sounds much less phantastic 135 years after it was written. Godwin expresses his vision of the future in the following words:

> Of all the sciences, natural or mechanical, which within the last half century have proceeded with such gigantic strides, chemistry is that which has advanced most rapidly. All the substances that nature presents, all that proceeds from earth or air, is analyzed by us into its original elements. Thus we have discovered, or

may discover, precisely what it is that nourishes the
human body. And it is surely no great stretch of the
faculty of anticipation, to say, that whatever man can
decompose, man will be able to compound. The food
that nourishes us, is composed of certain elements;
and wherever these elements can be found, human art
will hereafter discover the power of reducing them into a state capable of affording corporeal sustenance.
No good reason can be assigned, why that which produces animal nourishment, must have previously passed
through a process of animal or vegetable life. . . . Thus
it appears that, wherever earth, and water, and the
other original chemical substances may be found, there
human art may hereafter produce nourishment; and thus
we are presented with a real infinite series of increase
in the means of subsistence, to match Mr. Malthus's
geometrical ratio for the multiplication of mankind (4).

What is important is that Godwin recognized clearly that the
key factor in the Malthusian theory of ultimate stagnation was the
presence of a factor of production in fixed supply and that the entire chain of events could be altered if this factor could be eliminated. Like Marshall, Godwin looked to the sector of secondary
industry in which he expected the solution to the problem to lie.
He also considered that two further factors were of importance
for the conditions of economic growth, or as he called it, "the
perfectibility of mankind." One was technological progress, a
factor which though not denied by Malthus and Ricardo, was certainly underplayed by them. The other was an alteration of social relations, the subversion of the existing system of property
and government. This change he considered to be of even greater
importance than technological improvement or industrialization.
It was especially against this aspect of his theory that Malthus's
criticism was directed.

V

The discussion between Malthus and Godwin and the points de-
bated in this discussion sets the stage for many of the issues that
were to be raised by the members of the German historical school.
In so far as they held any "pure" economic theories at all, they
followed in the footsteps of the classical school. But their central viewpoint consisted in a rejection of pure economic theory
and its replacement by what later became to be called the "institutional" approach.

Secular economic growth manifests itself not in any single institution changing by itself, but only in the change of the entire
economic order. The members of the German historical school
outlined various systems of successive economic stages. These
stages were thought to represent generalized, but empirically
determined, forms of economic life through which a people had to
pass in order to experience economic growth. Five major systems of economic stages were developed by the writers of the
historical school. Their authors were Friedrich List, Bruno
Hildebrand, Karl Bücher, Gustav Schmoller, and Werner Sombart.
Two interrelated trends may be observed in tracing the development of the theory of economic stages historically from List to
Sombart. The earlier systems are much closer in general conception to the theories of English classical economics than the
later ones, and the later systems stress much more political and
general social characteristics than the earlier ones. This can
be seen best if we observe the basic principle of classification
which was used by each writer to distinguish one stage from the
next.

List's theory centers around differences in the organization of production. He, like later writers, as, for example, A. G. B. Fisher or Colin Clark, distinguishes between economic systems in which primary, secondary, or tertiary production predominate, and finds economic growth associated with an increasing share of secondary and, ultimately, tertiary industries. To be sure, List's terminology differs from that of his modern counterparts, but in principle, his distinction between the first two stages, "pastoral" and "peasant" economy, and his third stage "agri-cultural-manufacturing" economy, represents a distinction analogous to that made by them. He adds as a last stage that of an "agricultural-manufacturing-commercial" economy, thus exhibiting his belief that the increase of the tertiary sector is a sign of further economic progress. List's policy recommendations are based on this conception of progressive stages of productive organization. He favored industrialization and he proposed government support for industrialization, since he believed that this was the only method of increasing productivity of an agricultural economy. His justification for this theory was identical with the classical and neoclassical view, except that he tended to lay much greater stress on the potentialities of industry to lead to economic progress than did Ricardo or Malthus.

Bruno Hildebrand, whose theory of stages appeared in 1864, twenty-three years after that of List, still remains essentially within the confines of the classical theory. Unlike List, who placed primary emphasis on the organization of production as the chief factor, Hildebrand chooses the organization of distribution as the distinctive mark for his stages. He thus distinguishes between "natural" (barber) economy, money economy, and credit economy. He selects the organization of distribution and exchange,

because he feels this to be the most universally applicable criterion. But although the form of exchange of a society is, on the
whole, correlated with its level of productivity, this correlation
is, by no means, uniform and there exist important deviations.
Moreover, within each class there exist such great differences
in the level of productivity that Hildebrand's system is of little
use for purposes of a really insightful theory of growth. Its importance lies not so much in the positive contribution it makes,
but rather in Hildebrand's attempt to select factors in the economic life of people which are allegedly neutral from a cultural
standpoint. This led German historical economists to select criteria for distinguishing between stages which were not strictly
in the realm of economic organization.

Bücher's theory of economic stages appeared in 1893. In
many ways this system stands at the watershed of the older and
newer theories. Bücher's units are types of socio-economic
structures; he distinguishes between the closed domestic economy, the town economy, and the national economy. The criterion
of classification is the degree of division of labor, on the one hand,
and the complexity of social relations of each economic system,
on the other. Schmoller, who engaged in a long-drawn-out debate
with Bücher on the adequacy, degree of general applicability, and
priority of formulation of the theory, had published, in 1864, a
theory in which the political factor is the criterion of classification.
Schmoller's stages are similar to those of Bücher, but his system
of stages follows much more closely the forms of political development of Western Europe, and in particular of Germany, than does
Bücher's. In the place of Bücher's closed domestic economy,
Schmoller puts the village or manorial economy; this is followed
by the town economy, the territorial (or provincial) economy, and
finally the national economy.

There is no question that, in spite of the outward similarity of these two systems of economic stages, they exhibit several far-reaching differences. These differences become even sharper if the detailed descriptions of each stage are analyzed. Bücher remains in the realm of general social and economic structure, whereas Schmoller is interested primarily in the political forms dominating the various stages of economic life. This becomes clear by a comparison of Bücher's and Schmoller's description of the town economy. For Bücher, the town economy is one in which ideally, goods are produced on order for known customers and in which commodities pass directly from the producer to the consumer. The social nexus which dominates the economic life is one of primary or, at best, secondary social relations, and most exchange and production is carried on under conditions in which face-to-face relations predominate. For Schmoller, the town economy is characterized by the specialized development of communities with their own government, exempt from the jurisdiction of feudal manorial lords and subject directly to the crown or central territorial authority. It is clear that Bücher's definition is more generally applicable also to non-European peoples and that Schmoller's relates primarily to the growth of the economy of Western Europe and may have only limited relevance for some countries even in that portion of the world. Schmoller himself recognized these differences clearly when he wrote that Bücher's schema is more theoretical and tends to provide a yardstick for the comparison of different civilizations; that it starts from the division of labor and the organization of exchange and confines itself primarily to an analysis of social and economic institutions. His own system, Schmoller characterized as being primarily historical, as starting with political institutions and their economic policy, and as having the purpose not of generalization but of explanation of the economic life of different territorial units: village, town, city, nation (5).

If Schmoller's schema of economic stages was narrower in its applicability than those of his predecessors, that of his successor, Werner Sombart, was even narrower than Schmoller's. Sombart's stages are essentially stages of capitalism, and, as is well known, he is distinguished between early capitalism, high capitalism, and late capitalism. He also acknowledges a pre-capitalist stage before the full-scale development of capitalist society. But although Sombart's schema is applicable only to a part of Western Europe, he introduces a greater number of more complex variables than any of his predecessors. Capitalism and its various sub-forms are described as a social rather than an economic system, and attention is paid therefore not merely to economic, but also to political, social, and ideological factors. The conditions of economic progress are made dependent not merely — as List or Hildebrand had argued — on the development of productivity or forms of exchange and distribution, but on factors which, on the surface, appeared to be far removed from any economic impact, but which, in reality and upon closer inspection, are seen to have a profound influence on the form and nature of economic activity. Thus, the very real contribution of the German historical school, and, above all, of Bücher and Sombart, consisted in their having pointed to the noneconomic and the meta-economic factors which affect profoundly the conditions of economic progress. In so doing, they were forced to narrow the field within which their generalizations were applicable and thus they provided, at best, an explanation of those relatively few countries which had passed through the full cycle of capitalist development.

The main reason why their systems remained applicable to so few societies was due in part to their predominantly historical orientation, but also, in part to the relatively underdeveloped state of sociological theory in their days. Since that time new and wider concepts have been developed in social theory and more general propositions are possible. An example of the direction which the approach initiated by the German historical school might have taken is provided in Chapters II and III. There also a theory of stages of a sort is stipulated. But rather than concentrating on setting up a system of stages of economic activity embracing all human experience, the attempt is made to distinguish merely between two "stages," that preceding and that following a period of rapid economic advance. To this are added some comments on the nature of the transition. This schema, though narrower in a strictly historical sense than that of any writer of the German historical school, nevertheless, seems to have more general applicability than any of theirs. It may be hoped that further study along the lines tentatively laid out in these essays might lead to more valid insights into the general social framework within which economic growth occurs.

NOTES TO CHAPTER I

1. See Edgar Salin, Geschichte der Volkswirtschaftslehre, 2nd ed. (Berlin, 1929), p. 34.

2. See Trygve Haavelmo, A Study in the Theory of Economic Evolution (Amsterdam, 1954), pp. 9-12.

3. See Alfred Marshall, Principles of Economics, 8th edition (London, 1920), pp. 318-322.

4. William Godwin, Of Population (London, 1820), pp. 499-501. (Underscore added.)

5. See Gustav Schmoller, Umrisse und Untersuchungen zur Verfassungs-und Wirtschaftsgeschichte (Leipzig, 1898), pp. 59-60. A discussion of the various theories of economic stages is presented by Gertrud Kalveram, Die Theorien von den Wirtschaftsstufen (Leipzig, 1933), pp. 73-117.

2

SOCIAL STRUCTURE AND ECONOMIC GROWTH

I.

The widespread practical interest evoked in recent years in the conditions and problems of economic development, and in policies designed, so far as possible, to abolish poverty and want in many parts of the world has reinforced among economists the study of theoretical problems associated with economic growth. Economists have long been interested in the forces favoring economic progress. As W. W. Rostow recently pointed out, Adam Smith's Wealth of Nations gives great weight to the consideration of economic policies most conductive to economic growth, and the subsequent writings of the classical economists were, to a considerable extent, elaborations of some of these points (1). Smith and his immediate successors wrote at a time when a constant relation between economic theory and economic policy was considered both necessary and obvious. Since the middle of the last century, however, a body of economic theory began to establish itself which, on the one hand, to an ever-increasing degree, abstracted from the immediate policy implications to which it was subject, and on the other assumed human motivations and the social and cultural environment of economic activity as relatively rigid and unchanging

23

givens. In consequence, the further development of the theory of economic growth (with some notable exceptions, like the work of Joseph Schumpeter) tended to concentrate almost exclusively on the task of relating purely economic variables to one another and to disregard the political and social changes which accompanied the process of economic growth.

Even in present attempts at restating the basic framework of an economic theory of economic growth, the necessity of relating this theoretical framework to the cultural conditions and political needs of areas undergoing rapid economic change is sometimes underestimated or overlooked. Propositions which deal with the dependence of economic progress on the character of income distribution, the relative magnitude of savings, the impact of inflationary pressures, and the state of a country's balance of payments and terms of trade, are clearly relevant. Yet it must be recognized that even a secure knowledge of all these relationships is not enough, but only a beginning, for a theory which realistically deals with all the variables involved in the development process. And if economists specify (as they sometimes do) that, in addition to the various economic adjustments, a change in the social values cherished by a population is necessary, they make a statement which is true, but, on this level of generality, meaningless, for it cannot be translated into operational terms.

What is needed, therefore, is not merely a theory of economic growth in purely economic terms, but a theory relating economic development to cultural change. In view of the great uncertainties in the realm of theory which concerns itself with cultural change in general, it may be premature and, in terms of available scholarly resources, perhaps uneconomical even to attempt the statement of a general theory of economic development and cultural change. We may better begin by developing theoretical models for different types of societies and different types of transitions or movements from "traditional" to more "modern" forms of economic organization. The attempt to develop a general, universally valid, theory of economic and cultural change may lead into the impenetrable jungle in which have been lost so many who searched the way to the formulation of a general theory of history. The attempt to meet a more limited objective, the concentration on situations which are now clamoring for practical solution, may lead to the elaboration of a theoretical framework which may be useful not merely in providing a guide for present policy, but also in enlarging the boundaries of our general theoretical knowledge of social and economic change.

In pursuing this more limited objective one outstanding case presents itself, both because of its contemporary practical significance and its intrinsic theoretical interest. This is the problem of economic growth and associated cultural change in those countries which, in the official language of the United Nations and the United States Department of State, are designated as "underdeveloped." A Committee of Experts of the United Nations has defined such a country as one "in which per capita real income is low when compared with the per capita real income of the United States of America, Canada, Australasia, and Western Europe."

This definition not only specifies the variable which is considered most significant in measuring the level of economic advancement, but it also classifies a series of countries as advanced and others as underdeveloped. It further suggests that

the most important problem for investigation is the transition
from a state of "underdevelopment" to one of "development" or
"full development," and that other processes of economic change,
even if they are associated with an increase of income (that variable by which the level of development is measured), are not
necessarily relevant or may not be subject to the same regularities as the transition from economic backwardness to economic advancement.

If, moreover, instead of regarding this transition as a problem of economic growth in abstract, purely formal economic
terms, we center our attention on how underdeveloped, often
stagnating, economies reach a form of economic organization
which permits them to permanent indigenous economic growth,
we are invariably driven to consider (in addition to the formal
mechanisms of economic adjustment) the changes in culture and
social structure which this transition calls forth.   Instead of being concerned with the problem of economic growth in the most
general terms we are interested in elaborating a theoretical
model which permits us to analyze a process of transition from
a social system displaying one form of economic organization to
one displaying a different presumably "more advanced" economic organization.   This process involves not merely a reshaping
of the "economic order" but also a restructuring of social relations in general, or at least of those social relations which are
relevant to the performance of the productive and distributive
tasks of the society.

In practice, i.e., in a situation requiring the elaboration of a
development plan for a given country or region, this problem requires for its solution that the plan embrace not only prescrip-
tions for economic adjustments but also for the channeling of

associated cultural and social change. The United Nations Technical Assistance Administration, and other agencies participating in programs evolving development plans are conscious of this need, and technical missions going to underdeveloped countries include in addition to economists and engineers, also specialists in education, social welfare, and cultural anthropology. Their task is to advise on how economic planning may be directed into channels in which frictions with existing cultural and social forces will be minimized and incentives for the planned changes maximized. Owing to profound differences in the cultures of the various populations participating in economic development plans, a multitude of forms have been found in which cultural or social structural factors do affect economic growth. The great variety of actual conditions appears to make generalizations difficult.

Yet several attempts to generalize have been undertaken. These attempts were not specifically related to the elaboration of a general theory of economic development and cultural change, but rather to the development of a theory of capitalism — a problem which has close similarities to the one under consideration. Such a theory confines itself to propositions on the pattern of economic growth and associated social change under specific historical conditions encountered by the countries of the western world in the last three or four hundred years. The problem we are interested in is similar in scope. It has as its aim the attainment of some understanding of the functional interrelationship of economic and general social variables describing the transition from an economically "underdeveloped" to an "advanced" society. In pursuing our aim we will concentrate first on a description of the social structures which may be regarded as related

most closely to the economy in each of these two categories.
From the juxtaposition of these "types" we may learn something of the social processes which are associated with "economic development" in the sense in which that term is used here.

II.

If we consider, as is commonly done, that economic development is measured by the growth of per capita real output of a
society we must, to build a theory of development, determine the
functional interdependence between the level of per capita output
and other variables. In advanced economies these functional relations have been studied intensively by economists in the last
few decades under the general heading of "income analysis." A
set of theories were developed which relate the level of income
to such variables as investment, the rate of interest, the propen-
sities to consume and save, and the supply of money. These
theories, which have sometimes been considered as the main contribution of Keynes and his followers, have a definite but limited
relevance to our problem (3). The crucial aspect of a theory of
economic development — as distinguished from a theory of income and employment — is, as has been stressed earlier, the
need to explain the transition from a state of "underdevelopment"
to a state of "advancement." Now as was mentioned, the division
of certain areas of the globe into "underdeveloped" and "advanced"
areas according to the usual definitions is essentially arbitrary.
For example, the group of United Nations experts, whose definition
was quoted earlier, might have included Japan and the Soviet
Union with the United States, Canada, Australasia, and Western
Europe in the class "advanced countries." Certainly in compari-

son with countries like Haiti, or even Greece, these countries
are economically advanced, i.e., have higher per capita real
outputs.

But what we are driving at is more than a mere classification
in terms of this highly elusive measure, per capita output. If
different stages of economic development are associated with
different systems, each exhibiting a particular social structure
and culture, we must look for further criteria by which to separate economically "advanced" and "underdeveloped" countries.
These might be associated either with the country's economy, or
its culture and social system. We could, for example, specify
that in addition to a relatively higher level of per capita real output, an advanced country must have an economy based on capitalistic social relations, or a centralized, democratic government, or a monotheistic religion. Whether or not any of these
(or any other) variables should be included depends on their usefulness in providing a more adequate theoretical explanation of
economic progress.

Since we are interested in the components of different social
systems, each of which corresponds to a particular level of economic advancement, we may attempt to structure the relevant relationships in terms of the "pattern variables" as described by
Talcott Parsons in the attempt to state the basic factors comprising a framework in which entire social systems can be studied
and compared. In doing this we obtain a result in which the relation between what, on the surface, appears as purely economic
action to general behavioral typologies is exhibited (4). The contrast between economically advanced and underdeveloped societies
is reduced to its basic sociological foundation if the purely economic magnitudes are stated in terms of these pattern variables.

These variables, in other words, come to be regarded as the determinants, on the most generalized level of socially relevant behavior, of average real output of a society.

In making use of Professor Parsons' schema we must state quite clearly with what aspects of it we are concerned. As conceived by its author, it is a framework in which interrelations between variables relating to an entire social system (or certain parts of it) can be described analytically. In this analysis we are not attempting to describe all aspects of different social systems, or types of social systems. We are concerned only with those sets of action systems which pertain to a description of economically relevant behavior, i.e., behavior related to the production and distribution of goods and services. This does not imply a categorical rejection of a functional theory of culture and society, it merely means that with reference to the problems discussed in this paper, the question of the functional relations between all or most culture traits is left open, and special attention is given only to those aspects of social behavior which have significance for economic action, particularly as this action relates to conditions affecting changes in the output of goods and services achieved by a society.

In applying Professor Parsons' schema we may proceed as follows. He distinguishes five pattern alternatives of which three are immediately applicable to our problem: the choice between modalities of the social object (achievement versus ascription), the choice between types of value orientation standard (universalism versus particularism), and the definition of scope of interest in the object (specificity versus diffuseness). In applying these three pattern alternatives to the distinction between economies at different levels of advancement we observe that backward

economies exhibit usually (though not always) a lack of reliance
on achievement as a norm for acquiring economic goods. This
is not to say that in such societies achievement as a behavioral
norm is wholly excluded, but that it is limited, in the ideal-
typical case, to social objects which are not recognized as implying economic value. The clearest example of this is perhaps
provided by the form goods are distributed among certain primitive tribes, where kinship relations, i.e., ascriptive rather than
achieved status, determines the pattern of such distribution. But
the lack of achievement as a universally valid norm in determining the attainment of economic values is exhibited even in societies
which are far removed from the ideal-typical status of "primitiveness." For example, the principle of fair price, or the
prohibition of interest-taking, so widely prevalent in early medieval society, are instances of an ascriptive norm for the attainment of objectives in the economic field.

Achievement, on the other hand, has become the characteristic norm for assigning economic objects in an advanced society.
These societies usually have systems of formal education in
which different sets of specialized skills are taught and one of
the main trends discernible in educational systems of advanced
countries is the progressively greater emphasis on vocational
training. Another sign of the association of achievement as a
norm with economic advancement is the fact that one of the chief
problems of underdeveloped countries in the field of labor and industrial relations, as seen by experts from the more advanced
portions of the world, is the absence of an efficient system of
apprenticeship and vocational training on the job or in special
schools. This defect is of great practical consequence, since the
necessary training facilities often need to be supplied by the gov-

ernment and hence constitute a drain on funds which otherwise could be allocated to the creation of fixed capital. The relative scarcity of funds in the face of numerous possible and desirable investment alternatives brings into sharp focus the choices which must be made in their allocation between human and non-human resources. The fact that models of economic growth of advanced countries are usually stated only with explicit reference to capital investment and that costs of retraining individuals for new jobs are either considered negligible or forming an element of private rather than social costs, is further evidence that achievement as a norm is commonly taken for granted in economically advanced countries (5).

A second characteristic of underdeveloped economies is the prevalence of particularism in the distribution among performers of economically relevant tasks. Again we must not expect the principle of particularism in assigning economic roles to appear in complete purity in all societies on a low level of economic advancement but should rather regard the rule of this principle also as part of an ideal-type construct. But if we look for its manifestations in actual societies we can invariably draw our examples from economically backward societies, (for example, the caste system). In societies with more complex economies universalism usually prevails in the distribution of economic roles; in fact one might even go so far as to say that the principle of universalism is implicitly part of the definition of production in a theoretical framework determing the optimum, i.e., most rational and most efficient, allocation of resources.

The observation that ascriptive norms and a fairly high frequency of particularistic social relations is commonly associated with "primitiveness" is not new. Sir Henry Maine's proposition

33

that "the movement of the progressive societies has hitherto
been a movement from status to contract" is an expression in
different words of the observation that with economic growth
(and associated legal development) the ascriptive norms in a
highly particularistic context tend to be transferred to achievement norms in a wider universalistic context (6).

Thirdly, we observe that in economically backward societies
the performance of economically relevant tasks is typically diffuse. In part this is due to the low level of development in the
division of social labor, in part it is the result, and at the same
time the cause, of the low level of productivity. The ever more
precise description of a job is a requirement of modern complex
machine production. It is also the reason for the high per capita
output of an economy in which such complex production methods
are widely used. Thus, the specialization of tasks and the ever
finer division of social labor, require the development of the
principle of specificity in the allocation of roles. Specificity in
this sense is the outcome of rational planning, the result of the
combined application of the principles of universalism and achievement as a norm to economically relevant social situations.

It is important to note that the principle of specificity in the
allocation of economic roles is not confined to advanced societies.
There are certain areas of economic action in relatively "backward" societies, where the very fact of low per capita productivity leads to a high degree of specificity in the allocation of
certain service functions. This is especially true of the performance of domestic and similar personal services. The very
cheapness of human labor, a function of the low degree of technical development, coupled with the very great differences in the
distribution of wealth, are chiefly accountable for this. But there

is a fundamental difference in the social function of specificity as it affects the division of social labor in such a society and in an advanced society. In a society in which productivity has advanced sufficiently to make the concentration of relatively large amounts of wealth possible, whereas the remuneration of ordinary laborers is extremely low, the very difference in wealth and social status divides the society into groups or classes in which the status needs of the upper group require the proliferation of services rendered to it by members of the lower group. Thus the specificity of tasks is not based on economic needs, on demand determined by the productive organization of the society, but is a result of the attempt to buttress traditional patterns of social structure. In an advanced economy the various economic roles are highly specific, but the society, at the same time, is permeated with the principles of universalism and achievement which also determine what persons attain specific role positions in the society. The latter two principles are absent or only present to a slight degree in an economically underdeveloped society, and the specificity of an economic role is determined by an ascriptive norm, based on particularist principles of selection.

It is therefore clear that the explanation of the social-structural foundation of the contrast between an economically advanced and underdeveloped society requires that the three pattern alternatives be seen in combination and that their interrelations be stated. In this way the pattern variables cease to be simply descriptive symbols and become part of a functionally related framework. In order to make this relationship quite clear I shall exemplify the propositions elaborated in the preceding paragraphs in a perhaps oversimplified model.

One of the propositions generally accepted as valid by economists, at least since Adam Smith, is the statement that economic development, (an increase in average real output) is associated with an increasing degree of division of social labor. This
means that economic progress tends to lead gradually to a prevalence of specificity of productive tasks performed. With the
increase in the number and variety of functionally highly specific
tasks goes a certain "democratization" or "universalization" of
economic processes. For if a certain job in production requires
specialized intellectual or manual skills, it can only be filled
adequately by a person possessing those skills. Competition for
such positions therefore becomes open to all having certain objectively definable qualifications, rather than to those occupying
certain status positions in society. But the process of filling
productive jobs in this manner rather than by reason of traditional social rankings or family ties of a member of the society,
may be considered a significant aspect of the process of regu-
lating economic relations on the basis of achievement, rather
than ascription, which under the label "individualism" is asserted
to be a typical characteristic of modern industrial economies.

It remains now to take account of the fourth and fifth pattern
alternatives of Professor Parsons' schema, the gratification-
discipline dilemma (affectively versus affective neutrality) and
the private versus collectivity interest dilemma (self-orientation
versus collectivity orientation). These two sets of variables, it
will be noted, describe the orientation of an actor to the social
objects to which he is related. Since we are not concerned with
the total description of different social structures, but only with
identifying the functional relations between those variables which

exercise a determining influence on institutional patterns associated with different levels of economic advancement, we must ask
whether we can stipulate any regularities — or postulate any
characteristics in ideal types — which permit us to assign specific expressions in either of those orientations to societies on
different levels of economic advancement. There was a time
when one would have unhesitatingly stipulated ideal types — and
perhaps would even have declared them to be descriptions of real
situations — in which the degree of economic advancement is
correlated with the increase of affective neutrality. In other
words, the economic behavior of civilized man was considered
to be coldly rational; the primitive, naked savage was thought of
as an irrational child, his actions determined exclusively by his
immediate needs and his behavioral patterns to social objects
(human or nonhuman) purely or predominantly affective. This
theory, which until recently may have enjoyed a certain popularity among those who held vulgar notions of the cultural super-
iority of certain "races" has been proved completely false. The
degree of frequency of affective orientation toward social objects
is not demonstrably correlated with levels of economic advancement, and hence can not serve as a category by means of which
they can be classified. This set of pattern alternatives, although
of great relevance in describing and classifying certain structural
relations (for example those involving the frequency and intimacy
of contact between members of various social groups) has no relevance in sorting them out in terms of per capita productivity.

At first sight it may appear as if this would also hold true of
the private versus collectivity-orientation dichotomy. But the
significance of this set of pattern alternatives for the classification
of social structures according to the level of their economic ad-

vancement can easily be shown if we take into account the kinds
of group contacts characteristic of economies at different stages
of development. Let us, consider the "oriental" type of society
as showing the characteristics of the kind of underdeveloped
economy in which we are interested. Such a society has certain
features similar to the feudal society of medieval Europe. It
exhibits, moreover, great degrees of variation in the command
of economic goods on the parts of different actors. Although it
is not the economically least developed, since certain very folk-
like peoples may be considered as even less advanced economically, it is the society in the most strategic position from the
point of view of developmental theory and practice (7). Usually
it exhibits fairly pronounced and rigid structural relations and is
dominated by an elite which enjoys a monopoly of wealth, political
power, and education, the main status-conferring social elements.
With reference to economic values the members of this elite,
acting in performance of their social role, are predominatly
self-oriented. In contrast, members of the political, and to some
extent even the economic, elite in advanced countries exhibit
predominantly collectivity-oriented attitudes with reference to
economic goods.

In more concrete terms this can be stated as follows. In a
society in which the power of the central leader is paramount and
absolute the economic organization and economic legislation of
the society is designed, at least ideally, to serve the self-oriented
purposes of this leader. The clearest historical example of this
relation is perhaps the social and economic structure of ancient
Egypt. But this attitude is still prevalent in the theory and practice of divine kingship in the middle ages and reaches down at
least to Louis XIV of France, who expressed it in epigramatic

38

form with the words: "L'état c'est moi!"

Examples of the prevalence of self-orientation of members of the elite with relation to economic goods in economically little developed societies could be greatly multiplied. The almost proverbial corruption of European mercantilist, or some present-day Near Eastern governmental bureaucracies are cases in point. The series of revolutions which have racked many Latin American countries, did nothing to change the structural relations of social groups, but transferred political power from one set of actors to another set with the well-understood accompanying phenomenon that the newcomers could now use the freshly acquired political power to enrich themselves and their favorites.

In contract, governments in economically advanced countries, even with totalitarian constitutions, maintain collectivity oriented relations to economic goods or, at any rate, officially and publicly proclaim their adherence to the maxim that they exercise their function in the public interest and for the benefit of the public. Professor Parsons' also points to this characteristic of an economically advanced society when he shows that the technological requirements of a productive apparatus using highly complex and specialized machinery demands a degree of co-ordination in which the free exercise of self-interest tends to be destructive (8). But what holds true of the technical side of an economically advanced society is reflected also in its social relations, especially those relating to economic goods for the production and distribution of which the machines are employed. From the moment in which the chief aim of a fiscal measure is to affect the distribution of income rather than considerations of raising revenue, the principle of collectivity orientation has won over that of self-orientation in the conception by members of the political elite of their roles as legislators or public administrators.

But what is true on the "national" level, also holds for smaller groups. Compare the orientation of members of a medieval guild with that which tends to emerge more and more clearly in modern trade unions and employers associations. Although one would suspect that here is a field in which self-orientation with regard to economic values on the part of the members of these organizations meets with social approval, we find spokesmen of these groups representing their policies as measures designed to further social welfare, and in many instances this is not just camouflage or deceit. The experience during the war in which labor unions and employers organizations cooperated in the attempt to maintain stable price relationships exhibits the degree of collectivity orientation with relation to economic goods to which members of these organizations subscribed. Contrast this with the fact that during the Napoleonic wars French insurance companies issued policies against loss from smuggling enemy goods (9). Further evidence for the wide acceptance of community orientation in advanced countries is the progressive extension of social welfare legislation of different kinds. At the same time the very adoption of such legislation by the less advanced countries, a process which is doubtless fostered by the attempts of international agencies, such as the United Nations, the Food and Agriculture Organization or the International Labor Organization to induce all their members to accept the most extensive legislation in this field as a standard, meets, in many instances, with a fate wholly or largely destructive to the actual objectives of these laws. Though they may appear on the statute books of many countries they are usually disregarded, and when a political agitator or overly consciencious official demands their application, he is denounced not infrequently as a traitor, or at best a utopian dreamer out of touch with reality. The principal spokesmen for the non-applicability of many forms of social welfare legislation in under-developed countries are members of the business elite or even the governmental elite of that country. This gives a Janus-like character to a good deal of the economic and social legislation of underdeveloped countries. On paper the laws appear extremely "modern" and forward-looking but their actual implementation is so deficient that the "traditional" backward patterns of action are still paramount.

Thus we may add as a fourth characteristic to the variables discussed earlier, the fact that in economically less advanced societies there predominates an attitude of self-orientation with relation to economic goods, at least on the part of those actors who occupy positions in national or group elites, whereas in more highly advanced economies attitudes of collectivity-orientation predominate, or at least are highly valued. This result again is not independent of the other pattern alternatives. In an econo-mically little advanced society, small and simple organizations predominate, which, as Professor Parsons' points out are "typically managed with a high degree of particularism in the relations of persons in authority and their subordinates" (10). Whether these organizations are constituted for productive pur-poses or political power purposes the relations between subor-dinates and managers are similar. The roles of actors in each of the groups are subject to little change and the way in which a man-ager appraises his role is little different whether he interprets it as a political or an economic power position. One is boss of a firm to make money, one owns a plantation because this is the way to preserve one's wealth, one becomes a member of the political

elite to enrich oneself. Similarly the peasant or common laborer
regards the trader, the money lender, the planter and the public
official as persons who must be distrusted and who are out to
enrich themselves at the expense of the common people. Thus
particularism, the attainment of roles on the basis of ascription
and self-orientation with regard to economic values by members
of the political and economic elite are closely tied together in an
underdeveloped country and form mutually reinforcing parts of a
particular social configuration.

On the other hand, it is relatively easy to show that there exists
a close functional relationship between universalism as a principle
determining the selection of actors for particular economic roles
and the prevalence of community-orientation on the part of these
actors. This fact is not in contradiction with achievement as a
norm partial by determining the situational structural relations
of the members of a society. The positive content of achievement
attains, however, a different meaning as a consequence of whether
the valuation of a given role is weight with a self-oriented or collectivity-oriented dimension.

Summarizing the analysis of the social structural aspects of
the differentiation between "advanced" and "underdeveloped"
economies we may say that we would expect the former to exhibit
predominantly universalistic norms in determining the selection
process for the attainment of economically relevant roles; that
the roles themselves are functionally highly specific; that the
predominant norms by which the selection process for those roles
is regulated are based on the principle of achievement, or "performance, " and that the holders of positions in the power elite, and
even in other elites are expected to maintain collectivity oriented
relations to social objects of economic significance. In an under-

developed society, on the contrary, particularism, functional diffusion, and the principle of ascription predominate as regulators of social-structural relations especially in its economic dimension, and the orientation of actors in economically or politically influential roles is determined predominantly by considerations of their ego.

This theoretical structure clearly omits, in the general form in which it is stated here, the purely economic variables significant for an explanation of the rise of average real output, such as capital formation and changes in the relative shares of primary and secondary industries associated with economic development. On the other hand it explicitly introduces a set of factors which economists almost always neglect or underestimate and which may be regarded as the primary social determinants of economic progress. Their neglect by economists was perhaps due to the fact that they are "qualitative" and defy subjection to acknowledged standards of measurement. They can be stated therefore only as factors which are present to a greater or smaller degree and which have more or less significance for economic change.

III.

The main problem in the theory of economic growth which arises as a consequence of relating social-structural and cultural factors to economic variables is to determine the mechanisms by which the social structure of an underdeveloped country becomes altered and takes on the features which characterize an economically advanced country. In particular, economists may query whether this process of social change is autonomous or whether, and in what form, it is related to changes in the more purely economic

variables. In the analysis of past instances of economic growth,
notably in the attempt to develop a theory of capitalist dynamics,
the priority of non-economic variables has often been stressed,
and the often repeated statement that successful economic development requires a change in socially held values is doubtless to a
large extent derived from Max Weber's work on the influence of
a religious ethic on changing economic ideology and practice.

But the development of capitalist economies in western Europe
were unplanned autonomous movements, whereas the current
efforts to induce economic growth are consciously initiated and,
as far as possible, carefully planned, at least in their economic
aspects. The fundamental difference in developing a theory for
past and for present economic growth is that the former process
is an overall social process in which, a priori no causal primacy
can be assigned to any one or any one set of variables. As concerns
present instances of economic development, it is quite proper to
regard such factors as accumulation of (or mobilization of accumulated) capital, planned introduction of new skills and new work
techniques as the primary variables, and to regard adjustments in
the social structure as positive, negative or neutral "responses"
to these "stimuli." In other words, the governments of underdeveloped countries are resolved to plan for economic development and to carry out these plans to the extent of their abilities.
The impact of social and cultural factors consists thus not in
determining whether or not, or even in what form, economic growth
is to take place, but how easily and smoothly the objectives of a
development plan can be attained and what costs — not all of which
are strictly measurable in terms of money or other resources —
are involved in reaching the goals.

An example of the operation of the principle of self-orientation with regard to economic values will make this perhaps clearer. To the extent to which an elite in an underdeveloped country operates under the impact of this principle it will distort a developmental plan in a direction in which primarily its own economic ends are served. This may have the result that in a country which is dependent in its international accounts on the exportation of one or two key commodities, instead of greater diversification of production, technological improvement of the traditional cash crops will be envisaged as the main objective of the plan. In the short run this procedure may lead to a maximization of average gross income, but in the long run it may prevent the setting in motion of a genuine process of autonomous further growth. Instead of a loosening of social barriers and an increase of social mobility, we may witness a hardening of the social structure, which in the long run may be maintained only by further strengthening of particularistic patterns of exercising economic roles and perhaps an increase of formal legal sanctions placed upon the prescription that such roles can be achieved only by standards of ascription rather than achievement. The economic history of the Roman Empire from the early third century on is an example of how the mutual strengthening of these principles led, in the course of a little over two centuries, to a stagnating economy which became the easy prey of the invading barbarians.

Thus, apart from the case of autonomous, unplanned economic growth exemplified by western European capitalism, in which cultural and social-structural variables may be assumed to have created the conditions for economic change, in all those instances in which economic change is planned, the social structure and the culture imposes modifications of and, in some instances, barriers to the process of economic change.

A full theory of economic growth, as it applies to the transition of "underdeveloped" countries to a stage of "advancement" must, therefore include propositions regarding the mechanisms affecting change in the pattern variables referred to earlier. Some indications of this process and the institutions primarily affected have been suggested by Marion Levy (11). Professor Levy stresses three variables, two of which are clearly non-economic, which undergo change when a society passes from a traditional, or relatively non-industrialized, stage to one of high industrialization. He singles out, as a minimum, changes in the patterns of family organization, of production units, and of location of authority and responsibility. Change in the pattern of production units means simply that owing to technological changes or to alterations in the form and quantity of capital employed in the production process, a trend towards economic growth has become possible. It does not mean that such a trend is a necessary result since noticeable changes in the production functions of one or several branches of production may take place without influencing significantly total output. (This statement is nothing but a special case of Schumpeter's proposition that small, slow, piecemeal alterations do not constitute an "innovation" in the true sense.)

A change in the pattern of family organization has been observed to accompany all really far-reaching instances of economic growth. Its presence in the transition from a non-industrialized to an industrialized society may be postulated as an empirical generalization. It may even be argued that the abolition of certain aspects of the traditional joint family is necessary, because with them the demands of the new economic order could not be adequately met.

However, a change in the pattern of family organization, though necessary, is by itself not a sufficient factor to stimulate economic growth. The dissolution of traditional patterns of family organization may result simply in deep-going social disorganization, the creation of non-productive "marginal" individuals who cannot make a creative adjustment but suffer anomie or become criminals, gangsters or mentally maladjusted. These developments do not provide conditions favorable for economic growth. The fate of the family is determined by, rather than a determinant of, the process of rapid economic advancement.

Thus, of Professor Levy's three changing variables the pattern of production units is a necessary technical aspect of economic change in any form (and hence not an independent variable but rather a concept describing a system of functionally related economic variables affecting the level of output) and the pattern of family organization is clearly a dependent variable which changes as a consequence of alterations in the economic structure of a society. It is different with changes in the allocation of authority and responsibility. But stipulating changes in the pattern of authority and responsibility is only another way of saying that in order to have economic development we must have a change in the relative preponderance of different social classes. This change has occurred historically in western Europe and if the theorists of capitalism agree on anything, they agree on the fact that with the rise of capitalist production a new class or group of men — call them bourgeois, or entrepreneurs, or business men — attained first positions of leadership in the economy and later also in the political and other elites.

Basically the social structural aspects of economic development may thus be reduced to the following questions: 1) What particular

ways of deviant behavior in terms of the values of a "traditional,"
"non-industrialized" culture, will have the effect of altering a
system exhibiting general assent to standards of particularism,
functional diffuseness, ego-orientation on the part of the members
of the elite, and ascription as a principle of attaining economically
significant roles to a system in which primary emphasis is placed
on universalism, functional specificity, collectivity-orientation,
and achievement as a standard of attaining economic roles?
2) Which group of individuals in a given culture — provided its
characteristics can be stated in terms of meaningful generalizable
concepts — may and/or do become the carriers of this innovating
behavior? 3) Does this group arise as a consequence of peculiar
social-structural constellations of the culture in which it originates
or is it marginal to the culture in an ethnic, linguistic, religious
or other sociologically identifiable way?

   I do not pretend to be able to give final answers to any of these
questions, and, indeed, I doubt whether our present knowledge
of social change in general, and social change associated with
economic development in particular, provides us with sufficient
empirical data for clear and unmistakable answers. Nevertheless,
as concerns the first question, the following hypothetical propositions may be made for countries which are now in the most crucial
phase of their economic development: The major impetus to alter
the significant social, structural pattern variables is likely to
come from the plans for economic advancement already drawn up
and partially in course of implementation. The very needs of
economic advancement must bring about a gradual replacement
of ascription as a standard by achievement, and associated with this
a replacement of functional diffuseness by functional specificity
and particularism by universalism. The gradual dissolution of the

caste system in Indian factories is an example of this process.

A more elaborate example is provided by the experience with the implementation of plans for economic development in the Soviet Union. Beginning with the period of five-year plans, a process involving rapid economic growth was initiated. The magnitude of the task called for swift adjustment in personal behavior of large masses of men to new standards, and hence threatened to cause serious social disorganization. Rather than abandoning the plan, the Soviet leaders attempted to cope with socially disruptive processes by the introduction of an increasingly severe system of authoritarian controls, and, at the same time increased emphasis on achievement as a ladder of ascent and approval. The most extreme forms of wage incentive systems, stakhanovism, and other forms of "Socialist competition" were adopted. The logic of these two apparently contradictory types of policies consists in that they were designed to cope with a total situation in which conformity and non-conformity with the new standards were inextricably intermixed. Those who could not or did not want to conform were purged or coerced; to those who were ready to conform, high rewards for achievement were held out. Moreover the considerable differences in remuneration arising from the various forms of implementing "socialist competition" as well as the needs of the enforcement apparatus to operate with clear, specific directives, gave a strong inducement to the development and increasingly sharp categorization of functionally specific roles. This, in turn favored the strengthening of universalism as a principle for the recruitment of personnel, although the principle applied only to those who conformed, or at least were neutral.

Examples of this kind could probably be multiplied, and to the extent to which other instances of historical events following a similar pattern could be developed, the degree of confirmation of the hypothesis would be enhanced.

The answer, to the second and third questions could also be given in hypothetical form: Since there seems to exist a considerable body of empirical evidence that in presently underdeveloped countries economic leadership is concentrated among a group of people who also control political power, a reallocation of patterns of responsibility and authority demands a shift of political power from the present political elite to a different one and the simultaneous reshuffling of the status system of the society, so as to provide the new economic leadership with at least commensurate social influence and power as the old one. In some parts of the world this new leadership may be composed of immigrants from abroad, and in others it may be recruited from the native population, but in all cases it is likely that the individuals comprising the new elite will have occupied positions of ethnic, linguistic, or social marginality in the old society.

Partial confirmation for these two hypotheses must again be sought in the examination of historical instances, as well as contemporary events. The social convulsion accompanying the transition from pre-capitalist to capitalist economic organization would, if studied in detail, provide considerable evidence on the two hypotheses. The economic development of Japan, the Soviet Union, or Turkey, as well as the meaning of present-day social instability in many parts of Asia and Latin America might yield further evidence. It is impossible to do more, within the scope of this paper than to indicate the places where evidence can be found to confirm or disconfirm these hypotheses, or to throw light on factors which would make it necessary to modify them. A large field for research is open for social and economic historians as well as for social science analysts of contemporary events in underdeveloped countries. Only when the results of these investigations become available will we be able to indicate with greater certainty along what lines a theory of economic development and associated social and culture change must be formulated.

NOTES TO CHAPTER II

1. See W. W. Rostow, The Process of Economic Growth (New York, 1952), pp. 5-6.

2. United Nations, Measures for the Economic Development of Under-Developed Countries (New York, 1951), p. 3.

3. For an attempt to relate the theory of economic development to the theory of income and employment, see James S. Duesenberry, "Some Aspects of the Theory of Economic Development," in Explorations in Entrepreneurial History, Vol. 3, No. 2 (December, 1950), 63-102. A more recent statement introducing a series of variables which have received only scant attention by the Keynesians was recently made by Professor W. W. Rostow. See his work cited in footnote 1, especially chapters II to IV. This book although designed to present a study of economic growth in general is concerned almost exclusively with the phenomenon of economic growth in the western world, notably in Britain, during the last two centuries.

4. For the definition and theoretical explanation of pattern variables, see Talcott Parsons, The Social System (Glencoe, Ill., 1951), pp. 58-67.

5. Public education is, of course, also supported from public funds in advanced countries. But the high illiteracy rates and the need to support all or a substantial portion of vocational training from public funds in underdeveloped countries make the relative portion of investment in human resources there a heavier burden than in advanced countries.

6. See Sir Henry Sumner Maine, Ancient Law, (ed. by Sir Frederick Pollock) (New York, 1906), p. 165.

7. The process of economic development considered here is one of transition from one system of relative equilibrium to another, and the characteristic structural features of each system are demonstrably different from one another. At the same time there have been included in the class "economically underdeveloped society" several kinds of social structures, ranging from very folk-like to considerably more complex forms of organization which last, for lack of a better term, have been called "oriental" types of society. It is not denied that certain structural

differences between folk and "oriental" societies are fundamental. From some points of view, there are also structural differences between different types of "oriental" societies, which would prevent them to be lumped together in one group. It is clear, therefore, that the classification in the text is made purely for the purpose of tackling the problems posed in this essay and is not meant to be any generally applicable classification of social structures.

8. Parsons, op. cit., pp. 507-508.

9. See Eli F. Heckscher, The Continental System (Oxford, 1922), pp. 194-95 and 203.

10. Parsons, op. cit., p. 508.

11. See Marion J. Levy, "Some Sources of the Vulnerability of the Structures of Relatively Non-Industrialized Societies to those of Highly Industrialized Societies," in Bert F. Hoselitz, ed., The Progress of Underdeveloped Countries (Chicago, 1952), pp. 114-25.

3

A SOCIOLOGICAL APPROACH TO
ECONOMIC DEVELOPMENT

Although in recent years the study of economic development has made great advances, the mutual dependence between changes in economic activity and organization and in social structure is as yet relatively little explored. This is not due to the lack of recognition of the dependence of successful economic growth on social change. Ever since economists concerned themselves with problems of economic progress, but certainly since Marx stated in clear and unmistakable language that the origin and development of the capitalist mode of production was the outcome of the transformation of society resulting in the elevation of the bourgeoisie to the position of leading social class, the mutual interaction between social-structural change and economic development has been recognized. For, in spite of the many criticisms which have been levied against the Marxian theories, Marx's interpretation of capitalism as a social-economic system and of its changes as alterations in the relations between social classes and in the forms and organization of production has been quite generally accepted, even by his most ardent critics. The acceptance of these interrelations was doubtless aided by the spectacular economic progress made in capi-

53

talist countries. It may be said not unfairly that capitalism was the first socio-economic system under which the mass of the population was enabled to enjoy a level of consumption effectively elevated above that of sheer subsistence. Whereas the mass of people in all previous civilizations were periodically threatened with severe famines, epidemics, and other life-destroying scourges, the societies of Western Europe were able to raise productivity, and to advance scientific and technological knowledge sufficiently to escape living in the permanent shadow of fear of want.

This unique achievement of capitalist society in the field of technology, production, and economic organization has been so impressive that scholars were drawn to investigate its causes. They were motivated not merely by an interest in the social history of their own civilization, but also, especially in the last few decades, by the desire to derive general or generalizable sociological and economic propositions which would be applicable to societies in which economic growth was as yet stagnant and the level of economic advancement unsatisfactorily low. It is not surprising, therefore, that in the study of the interrelations between sociological and economic factors which are associated with economic development much attention was paid to the experience of the capitalist countries of the western world, and that scholars were inclined to draw heavily from that experience especially in their discussion of changes in social structure accompanying or conditioning economic growth. The thoughtful essay composed by five United Nations experts on Measures for the Economic Development of Underdeveloped Countries, discusses the necessary social arrangements which may be expected to lead to rapid economic development. In summary these men envisage

that economic development is only possible if the social relations
of underdeveloped countries are reformed so as to resemble those
of western capitalist countries (1). A similar viewpoint seems to
prevail among the experts of the International Bank for Recon-
struction and Development who have gone to underdeveloped
countries and helped work out plans for the economic advancement of these countries. It has been said that the procedure in
elaborating these plans was based on a relatively simple notions.
C. P. Kindleberger, in reviewing some of the reports of the
World Bank, had this to say:

> Essentially, however, these are essays in compara-
> tive statics. The missions bring to the underdeveloped
> country a notion of what a developed country is like.
> They observe the underdeveloped country. They sub-
> tract the latter from the former. The difference is a
> program. Most of the members of the missions come
> from developed countries with highly articulated in-
> stitutions for achieving social, economic, and poli-
> tical ends. Ethnocentricity leads inevitably to the con-
> clusion that the way to achieve the comparable levels
> of capital formation, productivity, and consumption
> is to duplicate these institutions...

Kindleberger's view is buttressed by a similar analysis by
J. J. Spengler who bases his evaluation not on three but on all
ten World Bank reports which had appeared by the middle of 1953
(3).

The number of references showing that views of this kind
are quite generally held could be greatly increased. Those who
hold these views envisage that the development of underdeveloped
countries depends not merely upon their adopting the economic
and technological procedures of the more advanced countries, but
also upon their coming to resemble them in social structure and,

sometimes even, in form of political organization. Perhaps the
most farreaching statement of this kind made by an American
scholar is contained in a recent book of Eugene Staley (4). This
work is based upon the proposition that the development of underdeveloped countries, in order to be successful, must be carried
on in the image of the United States and it develops policies of
how this can be done. Although Staley admits that the development of these countries may bring forth a world civilization
"in which the West's pioneering contribution to such human values
as freedom, individual dignity, and material welfare are preserved and combined with the cultural heritage of non-Western
peoples," his book leaves no doubt that the Western ingredient
in this cultural mixture would be predominant. This is exhibited
by such remarks as that "the social stirrings in underdeveloped
countries... in considerable part reflect Western ideals," that
the nationalisms of many countries in South Asia "have some of
their roots in the West's own cultural contributions," and many
other similar statements (5). The general impression evoked by
this book, therefore, is that if any successful development is to
take place the countries of Asia, Africa, and Latin America will
have to adopt social institutions and even social values resembl-
ing those of the West. In somewhat more down-to-earth terms
they will all have to become little Americas.

I discussed the writings of the United Nations experts, the
World Bank and Mr. Staley at such length not because they contain an explicit theory of the interrelations between social change
and economic growth, but because they show how generally and
almost unconsciously the assumption is made that modernization
and the adoption of western technology and forms of economic
activity require the simultaneous transformation of a society to

exhibit western social structure and even to assume most of the social values of the West. Yet there exist, so far as I am aware, two theories which attempt to provide a general theoretical explanation of this process of change. One is the Marxian theory of economic and social development, particularly under capitalism, and the other is the theory of social deviance which is built upon some propositions of modern social theory and, to the extent to which it relates to economic development, also on the work of Joseph Schumpeter.

The Marxian theory is too well known to require extensive restatement here. Its application to the economically underdeveloped countries is the work not so much of Marx himself, but of some of his followers. In brief outline this theory may be stated as follows: The underdeveloped countries contain societies which are either entirely pre-capitalist or, under the influence of capitalist imperialism, have adopted features of incipient capitalism. The extension of capitalist-imperialist dominance in the underdeveloped countries is inevitably supported by the native bourgeoisie and its political parties, by reformist middle class elements, and by intellectuals who see in this policy a means of bringing their societies under the complete dominance of the bourgeoisie. But the extension of capitalist and imperialist control in the colonial and dependent countries results in the expropriation of the masses of the people and the imposition of manifold barriers to the rising middle classes. This sows the seed of revolt which is expressed in its initial stages by the rise of national liberation movements led by the emerging bourgeoisie and middle class elements in these countries. The colonial bourgeoisie thus finds itself in an ambivalent situation. With respect to its own proletariat it is an exploiting class and hence allied with

the foreign imperialists; with respect to these imperialists themselves it is the chief carrier of nationalistic movements antagon-
istic to the imperialist interests of the great powers. This makes
the social situation in colonial and imperialistically exploited
countries more unstable, and improves the changes of success of
a revolutionary movement which will lead to the political and
social emancipatian of the masses, the overthrow of imperialist
power, and the chance for an unfettered development of the productive forces of the underdeveloped country. To be sure, there
is some debate as to whether all countries have to pass through a
stage of native capitalism in order to reach a socialist form of
social organization, or whether they can jump over this stage.
There is also some debate of whether the social revolutions in
underdeveloped countries are purely or even predominantly proletarian revolutions, or whether they may be based upon other
classes also, especially the poorer and middle peasants. But
these questions are problems of strategy and not of the general
theory applicable to the transition of a society from a situation
of economic backwardness to one of economic advancement.

Although this theory is expressed usually in terms of political struggles and hence abounds in a terminology of revolutionary strategy, the underlying conception is clear. Stripped of the
purely political and strategic appendages, it sees the economic
development of underdeveloped countries to be associated with a
series of social transformations which are identical with those
postulated by Marx for the countries of the West. This theory
postulates, therefore, a single-line process of social and economic development and states that, with minor deviations, all
societies must go through analogous transformations of social
structure in order to reach higher levels of productivity and economic organization.

Let us now turn to a brief examination of the theory of social deviance. Although deviance may occur in many fields of social action, we are concerned here primarily with deviant behavior in areas which are relevant to the production and distribution of goods and services. As I have shown elsewhere, we may characterize societies at different levels of economic development by describing them in terms of contrasting pairs of pattern variables as these were defined by Talcott Parsons (6). Economic development may then be considered as being associated with a transformation of social behavior from a form which in its economically relevant aspects it is oriented towards ascription, particularism and functional diffuseness to a form of social behavior oriented towards achievement, universalism, and functional specificity. In somewhat different terms this may be stated by saying that a society on a low level of economic development is characterized in the main by the following features: Economic roles are distributed on the basis of what status a person has rather than whether he has shown the necessary competence to fill the role; and economic relations in general, for example, exchanges of goods and services, are based often on traditionally prescribed and sanctioned acts and performances rather than on attempts to arrive at a balancing of values through bargaining or the use of a price mechanism. (An example of the principle of ascription in the realm of a system of exchanges is the medieval doctrine of just price.) But in the little advanced country the attainment of and selection for certain economic roles is based merely on ascription rather than achievement; the overall pattern of distribution of roles between classes of the society is particularistic rather than universalistic. Mobility is difficult or, in extreme cases, absent, both between social

groups, different professions, and often also between different
localities. A society with a strong and vigorous caste system
exhibits particularistic patterns in a clear form. Finally, the
types of economic roles performed in a society on a low level
of economic advancement are typically diffuse, whereas in a
developed economy they are, typically, highly specific. This is
an outcome of the increasing division of labor, which implies
greater and greater specialization of tasks as the economy develops. The primitive farmer does everything from producing
his crops, to building his house, fixing his implements and constructing roads and other means of transport and communications
whereas the modern worker in a factory or office is occupied
with one specific, often clearly circumscribed task to which he
devotes his full attention.

A society on a low level of economic development is, therefore, one in which productivity is low because division of labor
is little developed, in which the objectives of economic activity
are more commonly the maintenance or strengthening of status
relations, in which social and geographical mobility is low, and
in which the hard cake of custom determines the manner, and
often the effects, of economic performance. An economically
highly developed society, in contrast, is characterized by a
complex division of social labor, a relatively open social structure in which caste barriers are absent and class barriers not
unsurmountable, in which social roles and gains from economic
activity are distributed essentially on the basis of achievement,
and in which, therefore, innovation, the search for and exploitation of profitable market situations, and the ruthless pursuit of
self-interest without regard to the welfare of others is fully
sanctioned.

If we consider that societies with the characteristics described in the preceding paragraphs stand at the beginning and at the end of the process of economic development several additional questions are raised. What are the mechanisms which lead from one stage to the other? Is there only one path by which the transition may occur or are there several? Is the transition process continuous or discontinuous? What relationship, if any, exists between the form and nature of the transition process and the relative emphasis on different factors in the social structure that results? For even if we may assert that a developed economy exhibits in its economic roles orientations towards achievement, universalism, and functional specificity, we are making a very general statement and the concrete social relations which may be subsumed under this very general description may vary considerably. Nobody would deny that there exist significant differences in the social structures of Germany, Britain, Japan, and the United States, and yet all these countries are economically fairly highly developed and present economic role structures which are oriented toward achievement, universalism, and functional specificity.

The questions which we have posed would require, for a full answer, a discussion of such length as cannot be presented within the confines of this essay. Rather than attempting a full and detailed treatment, I shall present some thoughts which may be regarded as a general outline along which some answers may be obtained. Let us turn first to the question of the mechanism of transition from a stage of economic underdevelopment to one of advancement. Here the theory of social deviance has found its main application. Rather than stating it in a general form, I will concentrate on its applicability to the problem of economic deve-

62

lopment. Here also the influence of Schumpeter's analysis of the role of the innovating entrepreneur in economic growth has found wide and fruitful application (7).

The entrepreneur, especially the capitalistic entrepreneur as he was known in the economic history of late medieval and modern Europe, is regarded as the prototype of the social deviant. By definition he is an innovator, a finder and applier of new combinations and hence, in a society where innovation is at best tolerated but hardly carries high approval, anyone engaging in innovating behavior is, by this very fact, a deviant.

Now if the concept of deviance is to have any meaning, it cannot be interpreted as signifying simply behavior which is new, but it must imply that this set of innovating acts is opposed in some way to existing social norms or to approved forms of behavior. In other words, a deviant always engages in behavior which constitutes in a certain sense a breach of the existing order and is either contrary to, or at least not positively weighted in, the hierarchy of existing social values. If we apply this concept to the behavior displayed by businessmen and merchants in the course of the economic history of Western Europe, we find that we can speak of true or genuine deviance only in those periods in which entrepreneurial behavior did not belong in the category of social actions which were considered as constituting the "good life." Thus during the later Middle Ages, when the official Christian doctrine still regarded the practice of usury as objectionable, any person who engaged in financial entrepreneurship must be regarded as a deviant (8). Further evidence that in the Middle Ages financial activity may be considered to constitute deviant social behavior can be gained from the manner by which it spread among the peoples of Europe in the period from the ninth to the twelfth centuries. In Italy, in the period of Gothic and Langobard rule, moneylenders were almost all foreigners: Syrians, Byzantines, Jews. The same was true in the realm of Charlemagne. Later when Italians turned to financial entrepreneurship on a large scale, the Genoese and Pisans, Sienese and Florentines, who were all lumped together under the name of "Lombards," became the financial entrepreneurs in the countries north of the Alps (9).

Gradually in France, and later in Germany, England, and the Low Countries, native financiers arose and forms of economic activity which before had been almost exclusively carried on by foreigners became domesticated in one country after another. The earliest native financiers were surely still deviants. But at some point financial entrepreneurship must have lost its deviant character. Would we be justified to call moneylending in the Siena of the Buonsignori a form of deviant behavior? Can we say that the granting of vast public loans in Augsburg at the time of the Fugger was deviant behavior? Unambiguous answers to these questions are difficult because the practice of "usury" was as yet concentrated in only relatively few centers and the hierarchy of values was oriented still toward a largely self-sufficient economy dominated by agriculture. Moneylending loses its deviant characteristics clearly and unmistakably with the breakdown of the old medieval values in the period after the Renaissance. The famous letter of Calvin to Claude de Sachins of 1545 on the subject of usury constitutes a true landmark. Here a man whose words were acknowledged as an authoritative interpretation of the structure of values justified a form of action which hitherto had been considered sinful.

It has sometimes been held that Calvin's discussion of the

legitimacy of interest was not revolutionary, but merely an explicit statement of a situation which had been tacitly recognized and condoned by many canonist casuists long before his time. It is, of course, agreed that loans for interest were given among Christians before the Reformation, and precisely because such financial operations were practiced we can speak of deviant social behavior. But there is a vast difference between even the most latitudinarian interpretations of the casuists who yet viewed usury as, in principle, wicked, and the explicit acknowledgement of this as permissible in practice under the laws of Christian morality. This view has been stated excellently by Benjamin Nelson when he says that "not even the most accommodating of the casuists presumed at any time in the medieval period to call in question the historic assumption that the taking of usury was antithetical to the spirit of brotherhood," whereas in Calvin's teaching, "the specific gravity of the claim of brotherhood is radically altered by his support of the taking of interest and... impels our use of the phrase "Universal Otherhood" (10).

The case of usury exhibits the development of deviant social behavior and its eventual transformation into approved behavior. The role expectations of a leader since the 16th century presumes not only his desire for interest, but also attaches a positive valuation to this practice. A similar transition of valuation took place in the case of commerce, especially large-scale foreign commerce. Here the record is not as clear as in the case of usury because the prohibition of, and sanction against, usury was more explicit than against trade. Yet, if we compare the statements of some interpreters of medieval Christian morality, we find here also first a general antipathy to trade with a more permissive attitude later and finally full acceptance not only of the desirability of commerce but even of its character as a virtuous and God-pleasing occupation.

If we can explain the emergence of important new forms of economic activity through the presence of socially deviant behavior, we are immediately drawn to enquire how this pattern of change operated in other cases and whether or not we may stipulate the hypothesis that innovations in the economy leading to improved output and living standards are in all cases the consequence of social deviance. It appears that some of the fundamental attitudes and practices of capitalism originated in such a way. But once "capitalist modes of behavior" were generally accepted, how can the further development of capitalism be described as an outflow of deviance? Can we, for example, find a process of social change underlying the evolution of industrial capitalism similar to that which seems to have been present in the development of commercial and financial capitalism? This question is of paramount importance, because many underdeveloped countries today seem to have developed fairly well functioning commercial and financial enterprises, but appear to encounter their most serious difficulties in the development of industry and an industrial society.

One explanation which ties economic and social change to social deviance and the development of altered role expectations has been stated perhaps most clearly in a series of essays included in a "programmatic" volume published by the Harvard Research Center in Entrepreneurial History under the title Change and the Entrepreneur. I cannot go into a detailed exposition or criticism of the views expressed there. A critical evaluation of this line of reasoning has been published in an essay by Alexander Gerschenkron (11). If I understand him correctly, Gerschenkron directs

his criticism mainly against two related aspects of the theory:
its attempt to envisage every kind of change relevant in the study
of economic growth from one single angle, that of deviance from
role expectations and its failure to place sufficient emphasis on
other sources of change than the altered roles of entrepreneurial
or quasi-entrepreneurial individuals.

I believe that Gerschenkron's criticism of the entrepreneurial
approach shoots over its mark, especially in some of its appli-
cations to concrete cases. But I agree with him in that it would
be incorrect to place exclusive, and sometimes even primary,
emphasis on the entrepreneur. Even if we agree that social deviance and the alteration of role expectations was a significant
factor in the development of commercial and financial capitalism,
and — as I believe also in that of industrial capitalism - we still
must explain the precise mechanism which made these forms of
social deviance possible and we must not neglect the more specific aspects of the social structure and economy of the societies
in which these forms of deviance occurred.

I have indicated before that one of the processes by which social
deviance was introduced was the presence and growing participation of, what has been called, culturally marginal individuals.
The Jews and the Greeks were characteristically such culturally
marginal persons in the Middle Ages, and the Jews, at any rate,
seem to have retained characteristics of marginality all through
their history (12). As Park, the inventor of the concept and of
the significance of social marginality has stressed, marginal men
are — precisely because of their ambiguous position from a cultural, ethnic, or social standpoint — peculiarly suited to make
new creative adjustments in situations of change and, in the course
of this adjustment process, to develop genuine innovations in social

behavior. Although some of Park's very general propositions about marginality have been somewhat refined in the work of his students and followers, the theory of social marginality has not advanced enough to supply sufficient evidence for the role it may play in the explanation of instances of social deviance wherever they occur. Even if it is admitted that marginal individuals tend to make creative adjustments more often than to relapse into new or old orthodoxies, the record is not at all clear, and there are some students who warn us that marginal individuals are more prone than others to experience <u>anomie</u>, and thus to become carriers of trends leading towards social disorganization rather than to innovations of a creative type.

Moreover, even if we could establish that social deviance at least in its most important instances, is the result of the appearance of ethnically or socially marginal people, we would still have to consider the precise conditions of the natural and social environment which imposes limits to the kinds of deviance that may occur. Consider, for example, the development of industrial capitalism on a large scale in Britain during the eighteenth century. As concerns commercial and financial techniques, Genoa of the fourteenth or Florence of the fifteenth centuries, were almost as fully advanced as eighteenth century England. Why then did industrial capitalism develop in the latter but not in the former? The advance in science and technology in the intervening centuries had something to do with it. But there were still other factors which cannot be neglected, and which are even more important: the natural resources of the countries; their area and size of their populations; the place and function of the government; and perhaps, most important of all, the precise and detailed structure of class relations in the two societies.

The appearance of socially deviant behavior stimulated by the presence of ethnically or socially marginal individuals may thus be regarded as a necessary but, in most cases, not a sufficient cause for social change. Although this theory appears to advance our understanding of some of the major structural changes that occurred in the course of Western European economic development, it is based on too general concepts to provide either a full theoretical explanation of these changes or to allow application to less spectacular transformations in the field of economic activity and social organization. If we therefore state that changes in social structure associated with economic growth are an outflow of deviant social behavior, we make a statement which is true but so general that it becomes almost meaningless, since it tells us hardly anything about the process and mechanism of change but only about one of the general conditions under which it can take place.

In order to supplement the explanation of social change associated with economic growth which is provided by the theory of social deviance we must add other variables which are either aspects of, or impinge upon, the social structure. When I discussed the emergence of industrial capitalism in eighteenth century Britain I listed several such variables, and it appears to me that two are of especial relevance for our problem. One is the ratio between population and non-human natural resources of an area and the other is the degree of constraint exerted by a central political authority. The former has sometimes, somewhat loosely, been called also the man-land ratio, and the latter is an index of the presence of authorization tendencies in the political structure of a community.

It would appear at first sight that these variables are related only very tenuously to the social structure. But if we look at these variables not as general data describing a society but rather as factors impinging upon the manner and facility of economic development, we will soon find that they are closely related to social structures.

Consider first the man-land ratio. This is an expression of the density of population per resource unit at the beginning of the growth process. Stated in somewhat different terms, this variable indicates whether the growth process is primarily intrinsic, i.e., whether it consists primarily in an intensification of economic activity within a given geographical space, or whether it is primarily expansionist, i.e., whether it consists primarily in an extension of the economic "frontier" and a gradual spatial expansion of the area in which more advanced technology and economic organization are applied.

The process of capitalist development in the western world, as a whole, exhibits both the intrinsic and the expansionist growth patterns, and I consider it to be the chief merit of W. W. Rowtow's recent book, The Process of Economic Growth (13), to have shown not only the existence of these two patterns of economic development, but also to have related them to fluctuations in other variables of profound economic significance, such as prices, etc. But if the growth process of western capitalism as a whole may be said to exhibit both intrinsic and expansionist features, different countries in the Western world show wide variations. In some of them, for example, Germany, or Switzerland, intrinsic patterns are considerably more important than in other countries, such as, for example, the United States or Australia, where an extension of the frontier is a clear characteristic of the development process.

It would, of course, be a mistake to assume that any country or region whose economic history has been surveyed exhibits either an intrinsic or expansionist growth pattern in pure form. The case of Britain is an example where a neat balance between intrinsic and expansionist development prevailed. Although in the older industrial centers — London, Bristol, Sheffield, Birmingham, for example, — intrinsic patterns of development preponderated, several expansionist episodes are clearly discernible. The draining of the Fens must be regarded as a process of internal colonization; and the growth of coal and iron production in South Wales, North-East of England, and Scotland, as well as the development of cotton textile and other industries in the new industrial centers of Lancashire and elsewhere, which set in motion a vast movement of internal migration, must also be considered as an extension of the internal geographical frontier. Finally, in the nineteenth century, the growth of foreign investment and the impact of the returns from this investment had profound influences upon further British economic growth.

Switzerland and Germany, the Scandinavian countries and Belgium, but also France and even Japan display predominantly intrinsic patterns of growth. Some countries, like Belgium, Denmark, and Switzerland had only very limited possibilities of "internal colonization." But even some of the larger countries, such as France, were so evenly settled before the advent of the industrial revolution that relatively few "new" areas within the country's boundaries were opened up in the course of economic progress. Foreign investment and colonial expansion played a role, but were, on the whole, much more limited in scope than in Britain. To be sure, the acquisition of Korea and Taiwan, and later the domination of Manchuria by Japan, were important events influencing strongly the capacity of economic growth of the center. But the main growth process was concentrated on the homeland. With the exception of Hokkaido, whose new fields land-hungry peasants gobbled up during the past century, Japan's farm land has been fully exploited for centuries; and the growth of industry was superimposed upon the earlier domestic commerce and handicrafts of such cities as Tokyo (Edo), Osaka, Kyoto, and others, which even before the downfall of the shogunate had populations of around a million persons.

In contrast to these countries, the growth pattern of the United States, Canada, and Australia is profoundly different. It is not necessary to recount here in any detail the history of the settlement of North America or Australia, but the greatness of the population shifts and associated expansion of settlement may be gauged, if we recall that in 1860, on the eve of the vast industrial upsurge in the United States, Chicago had barely more than 100,000 inhabitants, Minneapolis, Cleveland, and Detroit were little more than villages, and Los Angeles, Denver and Seattle, only dots on a map. The importance of this development pattern for our purposes is not so much to point to the addition of vast areas to the economically effective area of a country, nor to derive inspiration from the heroism and romance of the westward movement. It is important rather because it depended on the appearance of a singular mass phenomenon: the willingness and, indeed, the eagerness of entire communities of persons to relinquish the security of familiar surroundings and to settle in the wilderness or almost-wilderness.

The significance of these differences in expansionist versus intrinsic patterns of development for the social structure of the countries which followed either of the two paths is twofold. In the first place, the settlement of a large area, unless achieved by forced migration or planned relocation of large populations, must depend upon an ideology holding out important rewards for the migrant. To leave one's home and to face the hardships and uncertainties of settling in a wilderness will only be undertaken by persons — whatever their own personal motives may be which impel them to follow such a course of action — who live in an intellectual climate where this type of venturesomeness and initiative is highly positively valued. But an ideology of this type is in itself the result of a social structure which is relatively open and in which vertical mobility is not made excessively difficult. It also is a social structure in which emphasis is placed on the attainment and possession of material goods and in which a man's worth is judged, at least in large part, by the command which he exercises over such goods. A second important feature is the impact exerted by an expanding pattern of economic development on the social structure. The migrants will almost invariably tend to set up social institutions in the newly settled areas identical with those they left behind. Although there may be some subordination of the newer parts of a country under the older ones, there will exist strong tendencies towards the establishment of relations of co-ordination. That is, the new portions of a country will develop a social hierarchy similar to that of the older portions and there will be strong forces at work to intermesh these social structures. Expansionism thus has the tendency of even further increasing the potentiality of vertical mobility in the social structure and to lead to a relatively high degree of equality in social relations (14).

Contrast this with the social relations which are associated with intrinsic development. Here the intensification of economic activity in a number of limited centers leads to a concentration of

population. The newly arriving persons come into a place in
which internal class relations are already well developed. The
new immigrants often only find a place at the periphery of the
society; they form the membership of the lowest layers of the proletariat and the lumpenproletariat. There are, of course, a few
newcomers who rise in the social scale, but the great mass of
the new immigrants is forced to content itself with positions on
the lower margin of the social structure. Moreover, there seems
to develop often a tendency, in situations where in-migration of
new proleterian or quasi-proletarian populations takes place,
for the existing social structure to take on greater rigidity. This
occurred to some extent in medieval European cities, where the
growth of the city through the influx of former serfs and other migrants from the countryside was accompanied by a strengthening
of the status and power of the urban patricians, and in several
countries of continental Europe with a predominantly intrinsic
pattern of economic development (e.g., Germany) where in the
course of the later nineteenth century class conflict tended to become more bitter than it had been before.

There is some connection between the impact of an intrinsic
or expansionist pattern of economic development on social structure and the degree of central guidance of, and responsibility for,
the development process. For it is clear, that the more open a
social structure and the less the inequality between the various
classes, the more widely diffused will be the locus of economically relevant decisions. On the other hand, the more strictly
hierarchical the class structure and the narrower the socially
dominant groups, the greater will normally be their responsibility
for such decisions. Thus when we speak of autonomous development — as against planned or induced development — we have in

mind a process in which economic growth is affected by a multitude of individual decisions, each made with primary reference to the objectives of the person making it. Autonomous development is thus found most frequently in societies which experienced some form of expansionist economic development, whereas planned development is found more often in societies which followed a pattern of intrinsic development. But there are, of course, some exceptions. Although the Swiss class structure is fairly rigid, economic development in Switzerland has been fairly autonomous and political processes have been democratic throughout. On the other hand, Russian economic development was certainly expansionist, but at the same time, highly planned and occurred in a country in which the political process was under a harsh centralized authoritarian regime. This is not the place to enter deeply in the explanation of these apparent exceptions, but it should be pointed out that both in Switzerland and in Russia very clear forms of political organization had been established before economic development (especially industrialization) on any significant scale occurred. Variations such as these constitute a confirmation of the proposition implied earlier that the ratio between population and natural resources at the beginning of the development process and the degree of centralization in decisions affecting it are independent variables.

Our analysis of interrelations between the process of economic growth and concomitant changes in social structure is furthered if we introduce these two additional variables and establish clearly their impact upon the class relations of a society. These variables perform a different role in our system than the pairs of pattern variables which were derived from Parsons. The pattern variables, as applied to social action in the fields of production and distribution, determine the distinctions between social roles and role expectations in societies on different levels of economic advancement. The former determine the more specific differences in the social structures of societies experiencing economic growth which are associated with different paths of economic development.

The introduction of these two additional variables permits, moreover, a more precise evaluation of the function performed by social deviance or the presence of marginal individuals as factors explaining social change. For the chances for certain forms of deviance to develop will depend, ceteris paribus, upon the flexibility and openness of the social structure and the degree of centralization and authoritarian control in the field of decision-making, especially of decisions relevant to economic growth. In fact, it is conceivable that, in the limiting cases, the degree of centralization and control of decision-making is so great that deviance is made impossible and that any change which does occur is the result of a change of objectives or aims of an elite controlling the allocation of resources and economic activities of the society. This process is not likely to occur very frequently, especially not in any very pure form, but there are instances on record where rapid economic development took place with an apparently astounding degree of "orderliness" and a minimum of social disorganization. The chief example which comes to mind is the experience of Japan. Another example, which, however, is much less well explored, is the rapid transformation of the New Zealand Maori economy in the period between 1840 and 1860. Before concluding this discussion I wish to say a few words about these processes of change.

In the few years after 1840 a fairly abrupt and quite spectacular

process of economic change occurred among the Maori. Raymond
Firth calls this stage in the economic history of the Maori one of
"enthusiastic adoption of culture forms" (15). Although statistical
data for the actual dimensions of economic growth of Maoriland
in that period are not available, we can judge the magnitude of it
when we consider that after 1846 a considerable number of flour
mills, each costing, on the average, rather more than Ł 200,
were built; that the Maori acquired ships with which they engaged
in coastal trade along the entire North Island of New Zealand;
that they expanded vastly the area under wheat, maize, potatoes
and kumara (a native type of sweet potato), and that they supplied
many white settlements with food. In addition they brought food
to Auckland whence it was transported to Australia and other
places abroad. Among some of the figures which Firth cites are
the following: In 1853, the Governor of New Zealand presented
a report in which he mentions the existence of ten flour mills in
a circle of fifty miles around Otawhao, at a total cost of Ł 2,720.
At Taupo a tribe erected another mill somewhat before 1855 at a
cost of between Ł 400 and Ł 500. In 1857, the Maori in the Bay
of Plenty area, some 8,000 people, had more than 3,000 acres of
land in wheat, 3,000 acres in potatoes, nearly 2,000 acres of
maize, and more than 1,000 acres of kumara. They owned nearly
1,000 horses, 200 head of cattle, 5,000 pigs, 4 water-powered
mills and 96 ploughs, as well as 43 coasting vessels averaging
some 20 tons each (16).

What interests us here especially is the mechanism by which
this transformation of the economic structure of the Maori was
accomplished. Although Firth's interest in studying this aspect
of Maori history is in identifying what culture traits will be adopted
more easily and earlier than others, his analysis nevertheless

throws light on the question of what happened to social relations
in the process of economic change. Discussing this period of
rapid economic growth he says that it "saw no diametrical alteration in the organization of productive effort or in the system of
distribution. Most of the fixed capital was owned communally,
by a tribe or smaller group of relatives, and controlled by the
chief of the hapu. In his hands also lay much of the direction of
the work in the community" (17). In another place, speaking
about the process of acculturation in general, and the lessons to
be learned from the Maori experience, Firth says that the order
of transmission of culture elements proceeds in the following
manner: material accessories (i. e. , the introduction of new or
better tools and instruments); technical processes; forms of organization; beliefs and institutions (18).

All this leads us to conclude that during the period of rapid
economic growth, beginning roughly in 1840, Maori social organization had not changed from what it had been in the old days. As
before the introduction of new tools and new work processes, the
society was organized in hapu and tribes with the chiefs occupying
a position of leadership within their groups; fixed capital was owned by the group communally, and each person's rights and duties
were derived from his position within the hapu or tribe. His
status depended upon that of his hapu, his labor was contributed
to the common objectives of the hapu, if flour mills and ships
were acquired by one or several hapu, it was the chiefs who acted
for the groups involved. Economic development among the Maori
in the period 1840-60 took place not through the appearance of
marginal individuals, nor through the development of socially deviant behavior, but through the elite's reinterpretation of objectives
which the society wished to attain. If before the introduction of

European technology, the competition among the Maori tribes turned around the elaborateness of meeting houses and fishing canoes, it now turned, in addition, around the possession of flour mills and coastal vessels; and if previously the splendor of a feast was measured by the amount of traditional foods consumed, it was now determined, in most cases, also by the abundance of European-type foods; the size and elaborateness of European-type houses of the chiefs; and other external objects which, in general, could only be obtained in exchange with whites and which required, therefore, the exertion of labor and the investment of savings in lines of production which would find a sale in Auckland and other towns inhabited by Europeans.

Here then, we encounter an instance of economic development which is associated with no significant change in social structure. The persons who held elite positions before, continue to hold them. Although they envisage the attainment of new goals, they are at the same time able to maintain their traditional position of leadership and, therefore, also to discourage or even make impossible the development of deviance. They continue to allocate labor and to organize the common efforts of the members of the community in the creation of capital. This centralized organization based on traditional leadership and kinship patterns makes the attainment of economic success in Maori society virtually impossible, except as a member of a hapu. The only forms of deviance for a Maori which had even a slight chance of lasting economic success were to settle in a white community, or to attach oneself to a mission. These were arduous and dangerous alternatives and it may be assumed that only relatively few Maori took this way out.

Thus, although the two decades after 1840 constitute a period of genuine economic development of the Maori, we find no signi-

ficant changes in their social structure. We also find that at the
end of this growth process they had attained a level of economic
organization which corresponded to that of peasant agriculture
with relatively small scale capital investments in the processing
and trading of the raw materials they produced. We can hardly
speak of any penetration of industry into Maori society and although they engaged in selling and buying, as well as transporting
their produce to market, we can hardly speak of any really extended commercial activity in which they engaged. Although,
from a purely technological standpoint, the capital they used was
the most modern available in the mid-nineteenth century, they
had no cities, no industry comparable with that of fourteenth century Flanders or Florence, and no commerce comparable with
that of seventeenth century Holland. And although economic advances of a rather startling kind were made by the Maori, we
still find that ascription, particularism, and even functional diffuseness tended to predominate as norms in the realm of economic
activity. It is interesting to speculate whether a further advance,
beyond the stage of a relatively rationalized agriculture could have
been taken by the Maori without sacrificing their social structure.
The answer is impossible to give, because the Maori wars of the
1860's and early 1870's not only decimated their numbers and dis-
posessed them of much of their land, but also forced them into
isolation and aloofness.

When the Maori emerged out of their partly self-imposed isolation in the last decades of the 19th century, New Zealand had
become the homeland of a European civilization. Some Maori
tried to continue in the old ways, but the resources they controlled were insufficient to allow the necessary savings to accumu-
late sufficient capital for competition with the economy of the

whites. Some other Maori tried to find ways and means of integrating themselves into the European society, and in these attempts they were forced to find entrance in an economy under universalistic achievement-oriented values, stressing functional specificity. Although their culture showed some power of survival even under the new conditions, a distinct Maori economy, as opposed to that of white New Zealanders, had virtually ceased to exist. As individuals some of them found places in the European economy, but wherever they preserved their distinctive groups, they remained peasants or fishermen whose basic level of economic activity — in spite of the adoption of some new technological devices — did not differ materially from the stage before the Maori wars (19).

The case of Japanese economic development, especially in its first stages, exhibits some features not dissimilar to those of the period of Maori economic history of the mid-nineteenth century. Here also a period of sudden and rapid economic growth was accomplished with almost no alteration in the social structure. To be sure, there were considerable changes in the power structure of the top group. Lower-rank samurai were the main carriers of the change. But their ascent to power, the deposition of the daimyos and, what is usually referred to as the abolition of feudalism, were acts of political transformation which left the main fabric of Japan's social structure largely unaffected. In spite of the great increase in wealth which Japanese merchants had enjoyed under the shogunate, and in spite of the relative empoverishment of the samurai and even many daimyos, the change towards a different form of economic organization did not originate through the action of deviant individuals or marginal men. The first stages in Japanese economic development must be regarded as having been brought about by a redefinition of the objectives of the society by a portion of the society's elite which was abler and more farsighted than those members of the elite who actually had held political power in Tokugawa Japan. It is admitted that in the later course of Japanese economic development there occurred a loosening of the rigidities in the old social structure, but all through the history of Japanese economic development many of the features of the original social hierarchy, if sometimes only in symbolic form, were maintained.

These two instances thus present us with examples of a mechanism of social change which differs from both the Marxian approach and that which I have called the "theory of social deviance." It is granted that the social structures of the Maori and the Japanese, before these people embarked on the road to economic change, embodied features which may be regarded as propitious for the alternatives taken (20). It is also granted that in both cases there existed important external stimuli to make the type of development which was followed, attractive, and there existed technological devices which could be adapted with relatively little difficulty to the needs of the developing economies. But in applying any theories derived from the analysis of historical experience to the problems of presently underdeveloped countries, the experience of the Maori and Japan is perhaps more pertinent than that of the European countries in which the modern economy was first evolved. It may, of course, be that social structures in some underdeveloped countries are such as to favour the development of social deviants or to allow wide scope for "creative adjustment" of marginal individuals. On the other hand, there may be situations, in which a reinterpretation of social objectives by already existing elites may be the dominant mechanism for setting the process of economic change in motion. Which particular form of social change is applicable to any one society can only be determined by a careful analysis of its social organization and the forces in it which tend to promote economic growth. If we do not prejudge the issues by applying ready-made theoretical formulations, and if we admit that various paths of growth and various patterns of social reorganization are possible we will be able to provide more appropriate theoretical guides for the sociological dimension in economic development.

NOTES TO CHAPTER III

1. United Nations, Measures for the Economic Development of Under-developed Countries, New York, pp. 13-16 (1951).

2. C. P. Kindleberger: "Review of The Economy of Turkey; The Economic Development of Guatemala; Report on Cuba," Review of Economics and Statistics. Vol. 34, No. 4 (Nov., 1952), pp. 391-92.

3. Joseph J. Spengler: "IBRD Mission Economic Growth Theory," American Economic Review, Vol. 44, No. 2 (May, 1954), pp. 586-87.

4. Eugene Staley: The Future of Under-developed Countries, (New York, 1954).

5. Ibid.: pp. 4, 21, 24, and passim.

6. See Chapter II above. On the pattern variables themselves and their definition, see Talcott Parsons, The Social System (Glencoe, Illinois, 1951), pp. 58 ff.

7. The "classical" statement of Schumpeter's theory of entrepreneurship is a passage in Die Theorie der wirtschaftlichen Entwicklung, 2nd ed. (Muenchen, 1926), pp. 110 ff. It is interesting to compare this with an exposition of this same theme made not long before his death. See Joseph A. Schumpeter: "Economic Theory and Entrepreneurial History" in Research Center in Entrepreneurial History, Change and the Entrepreneur (Cambridge, Mass., 1949), pp. 63-82. See also the essay by Arthur H. Cole: "An Approach to the Study of Entrepreneurship" in F. C. Lane and J. C. Riemersma: Enterprise and Secular Change (Homewood, Ill., 1953), pp. 181-195; especially the statement on p. 187, that "to study the "entrepreneur" is to study the central figure in modern economic history, and to my way of thinking, the central figure in economics."

8. On the canonist doctrine concerning usury see W. J. Ashley: An Introduction to English Economic History and Theory (New York, 1901), I, 126 ff., and in particular the stimulating essay by Benjamin N. Nelson, The Idea of Usury, (Princeton, 1949).

9. As concerns the later history of moneylending, especially in England, Ashley shows (op. cit., I, 195 ff.) that in the 12th century the Jews, in the 13th the Caursines, and in the 14th the Lombards controlled this type of business. Similarly in Germany, moneylending was, before the 13th century, almost entirely in the hands of Jews, Italians, and other foreigners. (Cf." R. Koetzchke: Grundzüge der deutschen Wirtschafts-geschichte bis zum 17. Jahrhundert (Leipzig, 1921), pp. 103 ff.

10. Nelson: op. cit., pp. 27-28 and 81.

11. Alexander Gerschenkron: "Social Attitudes, Entrepreneurship, and Economic Development," Explorations in Entrepreneurial History, Vol. 6, No. 1, (Oct. 1953), pp. 1-19, esp. pp. 2-6.

12. On the concept of "marginal man" and a more explicit discussion of cultural, ethnic, and social marginality see the work of Robert E. Park: Race and Culture (Glencoe, Ill., 1950), pp. 345-92, esp. pp. 345-56, and E. V. Stonequist: The Marginal Man: A Study in Personality and Culture Conflict, (New York, 1937).

13. Walter W. Rostow: The Process of Economic Growth (New York, 1952). For a more extensive discussion of these alternative patterns of economic growth and their impact see Chapter IV, below.

14. For the United States, a thesis similar to that stated here has been developed by F. J. Turner and his school, although they applied it primarily to political institutions rather than to social structure. The two are obviously interrelated. Cf.: F. J. Turner: The Frontier in American History, (New York, 1920).

15. Raymond Firth: Primitive Economics of the New Zealand Maori, (New York, 1929), pp. 456 f.

16. Firth: op. cit., pp. 458-459, and Great Britain, Parliamentary Papers. Further Papers Relating to the Affairs of New Zealand, 1954), p. 249. Firth gives many more data of a similar kind. Considering that only 30 to 49 years earlier the Maori lived mostly on kumara, some fern-roots, fish, and birds snared in the forests, as well as some berries and other plant products collected in the forest, the transformation of their mode of living, as well as the level of consumption was unquestionably drastic.

17. Firth: op. cit., p. 472. A hapu is a clan or extended family.

18. Ibid.: p. 474.

19. Firth: op. cit., p. 470. See also Raymond Firth: Elements of Social Organization, (New York, 1951), pp. 114-115. I owe much of my information about the Maori, in addition to Firth's works to the researches of my colleague Robert Merrill. Merrill's findings are as yet incomplete and, only published in part. Cf. R. S. Merrill, "Some Social and Cultural Influences on Economic Growth: The Case of the Maori." Journal of Economic History, Vol. 14, No. 4 (Winter, 1954), pp. 401-408. His final results may modify or correct some of the statements made in the text, but I believe, that they would, on the whole, rather confirm what is said there.

20. On Japanese social structure before the fall of the Shogunate and the features it exhibits which facilitated the kind of change which occurred, see Marion J. Levy, Jr.: "Contrasting Factors in the Modernization of China and Japan." Economic Development and Cultural Change, Vol. 2, No. 3, (Oct. 1953), pp. 161 ff.

4

PATTERNS OF ECONOMIC GROWTH*

Much of the current discussion of theories of economic growth is coloured by one of two factors which repeatedly crop up in the pertinent literature. The theoretical treatment of economic growth is either too strongly policy-oriented, or it is stated in an overly general form whose results are applicable only with difficulty, and often with grave reservations, to actual cases of economic growth.

Since the practical needs of policy-makers in the United Nations and its specialized agencies and in national governments concerned with developmental policies or colonial development have provided a strong impetus for the recent study of economic growth it is not surprising that the literature on this subject should have taken on a strong policy-oriented coloration. What the practitioners needed and continue to need are general guide-lines for their work. What they ask from the theorist, therefore, is to prescribe for them a series of relatively simple formulas which make up the basic equipment of the tool-kits they can take to the four corners of the world and from which they can select, as the situation demands, the appropriate item for application. The result of this situation has been the elaboration of a large amount of knowledge, the parts of which are little integrated. This is especially unfortunate since the concept of technical assistance has tended to embrace knowledge in many fields of social science and has brought together scholars and administrators in various fields and with varied technical competence.

The tendency of overgeneralization in growth theory has a somewhat different effect from the tendency of excessive policy-orientation. Its result has been to reduce the number of variables upon which the growth process was said to depend. A general model is easier to construct if the number of variables is small and the relations among them simple. But in such general models much of the variety of the historical experiences of the countries which underwent economic development is lost. Perhaps an example may make clear what I have in mind. Among the most highly developed countries today are Canada and Switzerland. To what extent can a theory of growth adequately explain the processes of economic development which took place in these two countries? To what extent could such a theory, even if it were sufficiently emaciated to account for the common features in the developmental processes of these two countries serve as an instrument of predicting trends of development in India?

I do not wish to deny that we may identify the bare bones of a theory which relates such variables as movements of population, accumulation of capital, technological change, and the generation of gross output in a quite general form. But in attempting to predict what changes we may expect in some presently under-developed country and what obstacles it is likely to encounter in its process of development, we must have models with more flesh and muscle than can be provided by a theory which relates a few very general variables in a purely abstract manner.

Yet it would be wrong to argue that if general models are inadequate we should turn to the other extreme and regard every case as quite unique. We cannot pretend to search for a theory of economic growth if the variables in each society are combined uniquely so as to allow us no other generalization but the trite observation that the only thing we can learn from history is that we can learn nothing from history. Such a position would be wrong simply because the purely economic relations which determine the growth process can be stated in a very general way.

The question is reduced then to asking how we can incorporate the role of governments and of social and cultural factors in a theory or theories of growth. Next it is necessary to ask what use can be made of the historical experience of countries which achieved a high level of economic performance and what insights can be gained from this experience. In what follows, I should like to outline at least some significant variables outside the field of economics which might be incorporated into theories of economic growth. The result is not a single, uniform theory of growth, but rather an array of typical situations conducive to growth. This is attained by constructing a series of "boxes," each of which may be obtained by describing contrasting conditions under which economic growth has occurred or may occur. I hope to show that these distinctions are meaningful, at least to the extent of providing us with a number of "boxes" into which actual cases can be placed rather than with an array of empty boxes.

I

The first problem to which we will address our attention is the ratio between population and the natural resources available to that population in the initial phase of the development process. That this ratio, which has sometimes somewhat inaccurately been called the "man-land-ratio," is of overriding importance is a platitude. Yet, it is strange that, in spite of its importance, it has attracted very little attention, apart from the obvious observation that some societies, as, for example, India, with a relatively high density of population in agriculture, face formidable difficulties of development on this account alone. If we turn to countries which have achieved a high level of economic performance, we find among them some which exhibited, at the time of their early growth, serious pressure of population upon resources, though perhaps not of the magnitude with which this phenomenon manifests itself in India, Java, or Egypt. On the other hand we find countries whose population was confronted with almost unlimited natural resources. Examples of the first type are Holland or Switzerland, and of the second the United States, Canada, or Australia.

Though in all these countries the problem of economic growth was solved by the accumulation of capital and the development of human skills which resulted in higher productivity of labour and capital, the actual processes by which the solution occurred differed substantially. If one were to apply Toynbeean language one would say that the challenge presented to the two kinds of society differed, though the over-all final objective to which the challenge pointed was similar.

In the United States and Canada, the problem was to bring vast idle resources under the control of society. In Switzerland and Holland, it consisted in developing the relatively scarce natural resources by combining them in optimal fashion with additional capital and the relatively most abundant resource, labour. Seen

from the standpoint of the accumulation of capital, the growth of
the new countries was essentially a process of widening capital.
In the older countries, it was one of deepening capital. Seen
from the standpoint of the development of the human factor, the
new countries had to find suitable methods for the extensive employment of labour, the older countries for the development of
high skills and the intensive application of labour. I propose to
call the first process of economic growth an expansionist process
and the second an intrinsic process of growth.

The distinction between expansionist and intrinsic patterns of
economic growth serves not merely to show that in each case
different optimum combinations of productive factors are likely
to prevail, but to relate each form of economic growth to non-
economic factors and institutions. Expansionist development implies the consecutive incorporation of new territory. This can
take place either through colonial settlement or by a process of
creating new political units which become politically and economically co-ordinated on a basis of equality with the older portions
of a country. What interests us here, above all, is not so much
the question of constitutional or power relations between different
provinces or parts of a country or empire, but rather the impact
of ideologies which accompanied expansionist patterns of growth.
Why did some societies seem to take up the challenge presented
by wide open spaces so much more easily than others? Why did
the farmers and settlers on the North American continent under-
take long journeys into the unknown in search for virgin land or
perhaps the pot of gold at the end of the rainbow? Why do we find,
on the other hand, societies in which migration occurs rarely and
is undertaken on a relatively large scale only in response to overwhelming pressures? Compare the degree of spatial mobility of the

early settler in the uplands of Virginia or New England with the Javanese who remains in his overcrowded village even though the neighbouring islands offer large stretches of good and fertile land.

I believe that the tendency to expansionist economic growth is a phenomenon which is as unusual in the history of the world as the development of modern Western technology and rational economic organization. This trend of development is not identical with empire-building as such. History knows many instances of empire-building from the time of the ancient Egyptians to the Muslim expansion over Nether Asia and North Africa, and the empires of Charles V and Napoleon. An explanation for these historical events has been suggested by Schumpeter in his famous essay on the "Sociology of Imperialism." The carrier of these expansionist ventures is a "machine of warriors created by the wars which required it, which now creates the wars it requires" (1). The object of this class is to maintain its elite position in society, and it can do so only by trying to pull its society behind it in the expansionist ventures which it unleashes. This ideology was foreign to the settlers of the North American continent. The star which led them across mountain and prairie was not the notion of empire-building. The need for a continental empire was a rationalization of the politicians, but what inspired the masses who settled the continent was the "myth of the garden," as Henry Nash Smith has called it (2).

To be sure, once an empire was conquered the spoils of the conquest accrued to the victors. The Muslim khalifs profited from the riches of Syria, Egypt, and the Maghreb, and the Catholic kings from the gold and silver mines of Mexico and Peru. But in all these instances the impetus given to expansion was either short-lived plunder or the force of a religious creed which upheld the élan of the conquerors. The goals of American, Canadian, and Australian settlers were different. They went not to conquer but to set up farmsteads and to form communities. The personal motives of migrants doubtless varied a good deal. Some went west because they felt that their domestic economic situation was hopeless. Others tried to solve by escape a family or personal difficulty with which they could not otherwise cope. Some ran away because they had been involved in a crime or other dishonest act; others again were religious fanatics or plain adventurers who were attracted by the romance and freedom of the frontier. But whatever the personal motives, they all became translated into analogous action through the operation of a powerful ideology according to which opportunity and success were to be found in the vast empty area towards which they felt themselves drawn as if by manifest destiny. In the long run this expectation of success was confirmed. The gradual settling of the American and Canadian west contributed not only to the maintenance and even the improvement of the already elevated real incomes of those who remained behind, but also, in the long run, to the prosperity of those who had travelled west themselves. Many did not experience this prosperity, but their children and grandchildren benefited from the endurance of the first settlers and became living proof that their sacrifices, their abstinence, had paid off. By the end of the nineteenth century much of the early romanticism of the westward movement had disappeared, but so had also the worst risks and hardships. In exchange, the grain and meats of the west, its minerals and fruits and its lumber had begun to conquer the markets of the world.

The result of this ideology of success was a society based on a strong sentiment of egalitarianism. To be sure, there exist class-distinctions in the countries with autonomous expansionist patterns of development, but they are less harsh and rigid there than elsewhere. Contrast the American or Canadian class-structure with the forms of social organization in countries which followed an intrinsic pattern of growth. Even where a society was founded originally on egalitarian principles its development was accompanied by a gradual tightening of the hierarchy of social structures. Take the medieval city state, the classical example of intrinsic economic growth. In the early twelfth century the citizens formed a group of brethren with equal rights and little difference in wealth. By the fifteenth century urban oligarchies controlled the fate of most city states in the economically more advanced portions of Europe, such as northern Italy, the Low Countries, the Hansa towns, and the towns of upper Germany (3). The new immigrant could find, in the vast number of cases, a place only on the lower margin of the social scale. Even today in Switzerland, a country with far-reaching democratic traditions, the social distance between workers and burghers, peasants and city magistrates, is much greater than in Anglo-Saxon North America, and the barriers against upward movement in the social scale are almost insurmountable.

II

In addition to the dichotomy between expansionist and intrinsic patterns of growth I wish to list two more distinctions which are of significance. The first relates to the degree of dependence upon one or more foreign countries experienced by a society in the course of its economic development. The second relates to the active role played by a country's government in stimulating and directing the process of economic growth.

I wish to propose first the dichotomy between countries with a "dominant" and those with a "satellitic" pattern of economic growth. The ideal case of a dominant pattern would be exhibited by a country with a fully autarchic economy, with no need to resort to foreign borrowing for purposes of capital accumulation, and without exports. At the other extreme we would have a society which draws all its capital for development from abroad and which develops only those branches of production whose output is entirely exported. If we further stipulate that all or the bulk of the capital imports come from one source and that all or the bulk of the exports go to one destination, we have the ideal-typical case of a country with a satellitic pattern of growth. It is obvious that neither of these two extremes is, or even can be, realized in practice. But we find some actual cases in which the one or the other extreme was or is approached more or less closely. Many countries began their economic growth as satellites to a foreign economy and gradually emancipated themselves, adopting a progressively more dominant pattern of economic growth. If we compare Canada of the 1880's with Canada of to-day we see this change clearly. The same change took place in the United States somewhat earlier, and in Australia somewhat later than in Canada.

But although larger countries endowed with relatively varied resources usually can and will make this change in the course of economic growth, some countries, especially some smaller ones, remain permanently in the position of a satellite. In other words, the distinction between satellitic and dominant patterns of economic growth is not necessarily correlated with low and high levels of economic development. On the contrary, the pure theory of international specialization leads to the conclusion that a country's real income is maximized if it specializes in the production of that commodity or set of commodities in which it has the greatest comparative advantage. Thus we would expect that, caeteris paribus, in a world free of absolutely insurmountable barriers to international trade, a country's real income could be increased by its engaging in more specialized production and thereby becoming more dependent upon the outside world. Yet this seems to be an outcome which most countries try to avoid.

I believe that the explanation for this behaviour lies in two facts. First the extraordinarily high risk which dependence on one or a few commodities as export staples is supposed to imply. A study of actual cases would reveal that, apart from serious depressions, these risks are, in general, exaggerated. But the vulnerability of a one-crop economy is increased if it depends for its foreign-exchange earnings not merely upon exporting one or a few staple products, but, in addition, upon marketing its exports in one country. It is this factor which establishes the satellitic character of an economy with respect to another and which is feared and resented because it is thought to facilitate, and even invite, political dependence and the possibility of "imperialistic" intervention and all that nasty word implies. The most typical satellitic economies are, therefore, also colonial countries where the "act of imperialism" preceded the establishment of a satellitic economy and those countries which are small and helpless and have, at various times of their existence, been subject to the impact of pound, franc, or dollar diplomacy.

Much more interesting than these countries which have, with few exceptions, not yet experienced a startling progress towards high levels of productivity and income, are other countries which

have shown considerable capacity for growth even though the pace
and magnitude of that growth depended upon events outside their
own boundaries and often upon the pace and magnitude of economic
growth in one or two other countries. A more or less permanent
satellitic pattern of development has been accepted and the best
has been made of it. This has shaped general attitudes in such a
country and endowed its population with a less rigorously nationalistic outlook than that of countries with dominant patterns of
economic growth.

Some evidence for this conclusion can perhaps be adduced by
referring to an historical event which may be regarded as having
exerted a serious and rather sudden shock upon several countries,
and by examining the response to that shock (4). In the late 1870's
the agriculture of most European countries was placed under severe
stress through the increasing flood of American grain. What was
their response? Some countries hastened to protect their own
agriculture, others refrained from doing so and tried to adjust
themselves to the new situation by taking advantage of it. The
countries which raised their tariff walls were Germany, France,
Italy, Spain, Portugal, Sweden, and Austria-Hungary. Those
that did not were Britain, Holland, Belgium, Switzerland, and
Denmark. With the exception of Britain, which is in a special
class, since the decision to admit foreign agricultural products
free of duty had already been made some thirty years earlier,
all the countries that tried to adjust themselves to the new situation
were small countries whose economic growth already, before this
large-scale inflow of American grain, had been adapted to fit into
the trading patterns of the larger countries surrounding them.
The two most notable instances are Switzerland and Denmark.
They both accepted the new cheap grains and altered the general

composition of their agricultural output by substituting the production and export of high-grade foodstuffs, (bacon, eggs, and dairy products) for the production of domestic grain. In other words, the adjustment to the new situation increased their dependence upon foreign markets. Since Denmark's economic progress depended clearly, under these conditions, upon its finding a market for its products in either Britain or Germany, the satellitic character of its growth was made more definite. Switzerland's dependence upon any one or two foreign countries was less pronounced, but even so almost 56 per cent of its total exports in the 1890's went to the three main trading partners: Germany, France, and Britain. Swiss exports consisted not merely of agricultural products, but chiefly of watches and other forms of complex machinery. An analysis of the commodities making up Swiss export trade yields, however, the unmistakable result that its productive effort was directed largely to the supplying of certain specialized goods which it was particularly fitted to produce. The development of the Swiss economy in the nineteenth century could not have taken place in the form in which it actually did occur, but for the capacity of the Swiss to adjust their productive pattern to the needs and opportunities of the countries surrounding them. Hence the Swiss economy, like the Danish, tended to exhibit a satellitic pattern of growth.

The very different response of Germany and France to the inflow of American grain confirms the view that they were engaged in a dominant pattern of growth. On the surface there is no reason why they should not have followed the British example and imported agricultural commodities free. In fact this course of action was urged in both countries by certain sections of public opinion. I am not overlooking the fact that pressures against imitating the British

example were overwhelming both in France and Germany, but
why could these pressures be exerted in their full strength? Why
was resistance to the protectionists so weak and based essentially
on doctrinaire reasoning rather than the claims of a sound economic policy? I believe that the atmosphere prevailing in each of
these two countries which were engaged in dominant growth induced representatives of the most varied political and ideological
persuasions to favour a pattern of simultaneous vigorous development of all branches of productive activity as a necessary prerequisite of "balanced" economic progress. In other words, the general
orientation prevailing with respect to developing the country's resources tended to favour a high degree of self-sufficiency and self-
reliance in economic performance.

III

The distinction between dominant and satellitic patterns of
growth takes on particular importance if we consider a further
dichotomy, that between autonomous and induced economic development. This dichotomy relates to the role of active governmental
intervention in the development process. In characterizing the
two types of patterns, here again we could stipulate ideal types
which represent extremes not actually realized in practice, but
at best approached more or less closely. The ideal autonomous
pattern of growth is one in which all decisions affecting economic
growth are made by individuals other than those holding political
power. In other words, the ideal of an autonomous pattern is
realized in the entirely liberal state in which the system of political checks and balances within the government is supplemented
by a system of checks and balances in the distribution of social tasks.

Except in very primitive societies, it is wealth, education, and political power that confer the highest status. The ideal form of the liberal state is based upon the assumption that crucial decisions in each of these three fields of social action will be exercised by a different social group or class, and that decisions affecting economic "values" will be made essentially on the basis of self-interest. S system which operates in this way fulfils in practical performance the classical model according to which autonomous economic growth, that is, an increase in output and, with it, material welfare, results from each person's pursuing his self-interest and in this way unconsciously, as it were, contributing to the common good. It will be remembered that an important aspect of the Marxian criticism of "bourgeois capitalism" was based on the assertion that this separation did not exist, or existed only in appearance, and that in Friedrich Engels' words, "the modern state, no matter what its form, is essentially a capitalist machine, the state of the capitalists (5).

At the other extreme is the social system in which economic decisions are entirely determined by a central planning-agency. Ideally such a system would imply distribution not by means of the price mechanism but by a system of rationing or some similar form of direct allocation. All economic growth in such a system would be strictly induced, that is, provided for and planned by a central authority.

No contention is made that these ideal types of distributing decision-making functions among holders of political power and independent private individuals are realized anywhere in practice. Even in a country with so extensive a degree of planning as the U.S.S.R. some autonomy in making economic decisions is maintained. Indeed, it may be argued that a fully planned system would impose such rigidities as to make effective economic growth almost impossible. However, actual cases again come more or less close to the ideal types. Certainly most of the economic growth in the nineteenth century occurred in the form of autonomous development, whereas in the present century increasing reliance is placed upon patterns of induced development. The chief argument in favour of induced development is that it makes for more rapid economic growth. Bronfenbrenner has presented, in a recent article, three models exhibiting the relative rates of growth of systems with autonomous and induced growth (6). He concludes that, on theoretical grounds, growth rates are higher in a system in which all capital is confiscated and investment decisions centrally made than in a system in which investment decisions are made by private individuals. We have, moreover, some empirical evidence which would tend to confirm his conclusion. Kuznets has recently collected a series of long-term growth rates for various countries, covering the last three decades of the nineteenth and for the first four or five decades of the twentieth century (7). Of the fourteen countries for which Kuznets presents data only one, Japan, experienced induced growth. Japanese rates of growth are higher than those of other countries, whether computed on an over-all basis or on a per capita basis. If the seventy-year period is broken down into sub-periods of approximately two decades each, Japan also leads the field. There are, however, several sub-periods in which the rates in some countries with autonomous patterns of growth come close to of Japan. For example, the two decades in the United States from 1878 to 1898, in Canada from 1880 to 1900, in Sweden from 1890 to 1910, in Germany and Italy from 1870 to 1890, exhibit over-all (though sometimes not per capita) rates close to those of Japan. Unfortunately no reliable information is available on rates in the Soviet Union, but the researches of Gregory Grossman seem to indicate that in the period from 1928 to 1937 over-all rates amounted to between 90 and 100 per cent per decade (8). Even if these data should prove exaggerated, and we accept the lower estimates of Colin Clark, Jasny, and Wyler, which fluctuate around 5 per cent per annum, the compounded rate of decennial growth would amount to 63 per cent, which is higher than any rate recorded in a country with an autonomous pattern of development. The highest rate ever reached by Japan was 60.7 per cent per decade, by the United States 52.4 per cent, by Canada 45.7 per cent, and by Germany 44.5 per cent. All other countries discussed by Kuznets had rates of less than 40 per cent per decade. It is questionable whether a rate such as that of Soviet Russia can be maintained for long in any country, but if it is true — as is sometimes maintained — that the chief diffi-culty of countries that are at present underdeveloped is in over-coming an initial hump, then they would be more likely to gather momentum by induced growth than by autonomous growth.

I have already pointed out that pure induced and pure autono-mous patterns of growth do not exist in practice. This brings up the delicate question of where to draw the line between them. The types of inducements to growth may vary with the times and the circumstances. A programme of tariff protection may, under certain conditions, provide an overwhelmingly powerful induce-ment for private investment decisions in the direction of a high rate of growth. At other times and under different conditions, such a programme may have only negligible effects. The same holds for other policies short of out-and-out planning. For example, many persons make Germany's currency reform of 1948 respon-sible for initiating a period of rapid growth in that country. Another instance which has sometimes been cited is the liberalization of trade and the diminution of governmental intervention under Napoleon III in France which were associated with a noticeable speeding up of economic growth in that country (9).

These instances suggest another difficulty in classifying countries according to this criterion. Governmental practice may not coincide with the norms stipulated for the conduct of the political authorities. In other words, the relations between government and private individuals in the economic sphere may be so conceived as to leave, ideally, all significant decisions to the private individuals, yet government may impose narrow limits within which private initiative may be exercised or may use various forms of subsidies, so that, in practice, the process of growth depends primarily upon the government's "inducements" rather than upon autonomous private decisions. This situation can become even more complex since governmental paternalism may extend to areas other than economic life. It is conceivable that, on the one hand, a government may be quite autocratic in the political sphere and yet leave a relatively high degree of freedom to private economic decisions. On the other hand, it is possible for a government to employ relatively few constraints in the political sphere and engage simultaneously in a programme of extensive direct and indirect subsidization in the economic sphere. These differences in governmental behaviour in different arenas of social life and this contradiction between theory and practice with respect to governmental intervention in the economic process has caused and continues to cause some confusion in distinguishing autonomous from induced patterns of growth.

In view of the autocratic political tendencies of Imperial Germany in the forty years before the First World War, it is often asserted that in that country economic growth was largely induced by the government. Though the German government pursued a vigorous economic policy, its over-all intervention in the free market was not more extensive, and perhaps less so, than that of most Western governments at that time. Even the much touted social-security legislation of Bismarck, which in radical-liberal circles was regarded as rank socialism, was much milder than many social-security programmes which are currently thought to be perfectly reconcilable with a system of capitalistic free enterprise. If, therefore, we draw our line of distinction between induced and autonomous patterns of growth in such a way as to include in the former only those types of governmental action which have the aim of consciously allocating productive factors in a specified direction, the policies of almost all governments in the period before 1914 should be regarded as permitting an autonomous process of growth.

If we go back still farther in time than the early nineteenth century and consider policies of European states in the mercantilist period, we are faced with a more complex and difficult situation. The mercantilist policies of different countries have sometimes been distinguished in that in some of them, especially in Britain and Holland, the regulation of commerce was seen as the principal economic goal of mercantilism, whereas in others, notably in France and some of the German states, the stimulation of manufactures was considered to be the chief aim of governmental policy in the economic sphere. Though this distinction is perhaps exaggerated, the emphasis in the policy-orientation of the economic literature of the seventeenth and eighteenth centuries in Britain, Holland, France, and Germany tends to lend some validity to this distinction. But although continental governments were eager to foster manufacturing, they were only to a very limited extent engaged in direct industrial "planning." To be sure, the French government and some German principalities established state-owned enterprises, but the main reliance for industrial development was on private decisions. The administrations of Laffemas and Colbert, the two chief protagonists of the pro-industrialist policy of France, were filled with attempts to induce private individuals to engage in, or increase the scale of, manufacturing. The government offered premiums and prizes, exemptions from taxation and subsidies in cash, to stimulate private entrepreneurship in industry. Here we have an instance where ideally the decisions for growth were entrusted to private persons acting presumably in pursuit of self-interest, yet where actually a very active role was taken by government in stimulating and channelling private actions in directions selected by the political elite. This was a case of governmental paternalism in the economic sphere which produced a tradition of dependence upon governmental aid on the part of industrial entrepreneurs and which had the effect of weakening and even stunting private initiative when the hand of government was withdrawn. This appears to be one of the reasons why, with the introduction of more liberal economic policies during the Second Empire, French industrial growth never reached the pace of British and German, and why even then it had to be buttressed by an elaborate system of investment banking in which many of the crucial investment decisions were made by bankers rather than by industrialists (10).

IV

We now have assembled all the building-blocks for our array of boxes. Combining the three sets of dichotomies with one another we obtain eight possible types of cases or ideal types. To each type can be assigned, on a priori grounds at least, some country or countries whose developmental experience or possibilities for growth correspond most closely to that type. A list of these eight types would contain the following cases:

1. Expansionist, dominant, autonomous: the United States, from 1830 to 1890.

2. Expansionist, dominant, induced: the Soviet Union, from 1928 to the present.

3. Expansionist, satellitic, autonomous: Australia to 1914 or Canada to 1900.

4. Expansionist, satellitic, induced: Manchuria under Japanese control, and perhaps some areas in Africa now undergoing economic development, for example the Belgian Congo or the Portugese colonies.

5. Intrinsic, dominant, autonomous: nineteenth-century France or Germany.

6. Intrinsic, dominant, induced: Japan, or Turkey since 1922.

7. Intrinsic, satellitic, autonomous: Denmark or Switzerland before 1914.

8. Intrinsic, satellitic, induced: the so-called "people's democracies" in Eastern Europe.

Of the countries in Asia we would expect India to try to follow a pattern of intrinsic, dominant, and probably strongly induced development, and countries like Burma and Thailand, and perhaps also the Phillippines, all of them having large areas that can be made fit for settlement at relatively low cost, to follow an expansionist, induced pattern. The degree of dominance in the different countries may vary. Many parts of Latin America will probably remain dependent upon the United States and other countries of the West for a long time, in spite of vigorous efforts to attain greater self-sufficiency, whereas in South and East Asia, for cultural and political reasons, tendencies towards dominant — possibly regionally dominant — growth patterns will be attempted.

The first result of our system of classification is thus to distinguish more clearly between different patterns of development which may be prescribed for different underdeveloped countries by their resources, role of government, and interaction with the world economy. But the classification provides us with more than merely a way of distinguishing cases of development more neatly. It has independent value in permitting more accurate insights into the functional relations between economic and non-economic variables determining the rate and direction of economic growth. Its value may be exemplified by two instances, one drawn from the historical experience of western Europe and the other relating to alternative means of achieving the developmental objectives of a region little developed economically.

First let us examine whether the procedures of this paper permit us to cast more light on a problem which has provoked some dispute among social historians. I refer to the economic decline of northern Italy in the post-Renaissance period, but especially in the late sixteenth and seventeenth centuries. There exist, of course, several explanations for this phenomenon. Some attribute it primarily to the failure of nerve, the stunting of the spirit of enterprise, and the flaccidity of morals resulting from the corrupting influence of wealth and luxury. Others attribute it mainly to the shift of the geographical centres of world commerce and the impact of the discoveries which moved the key trading-routes from

the Mediterranean to the Atlantic. Others again attribute it
largely to the impact of a religious ethic which prevented the
development of industrialism organized on capitalistic lines,
though it had not been able to thwart fully the realization of
human cupidity in the form of gains derived from commerce and
financial speculation (11). Some writers have assigned more
importance to one factor than to the others; but they have all
been stressed with different emphasis. The problem has attracted attention because its explanation bears a crucial relation
to the explanation of the social and economic conditions of capitalistic development and with it of the economic growth typical
of the Western world.

There is no question but that the discoveries and the opening
up of new trade routes, markets, and sources of supply profoundly
affected the economy of the northern Italian cities. Adjustments
of a far-reaching nature were required, and only imaginative,
inventive individuals could make them. Why did the north Italian
cities fail so miserably to adapt themselves to the changed conditions of the world economy? Why did a people which had produced imaginative and venturesome individuals for centuries all of
a sudden cease to produce them, or at least fail to enable them to
attain positions in society in which their impact could be felt?
Posing the problem in this fashion we may find a clue to a more
satisfactory solution.

The Italian city states of the Middle Ages and the Renaissance
had small territories with relatively poor natural resources. Under
these conditions virtually the only avenue to the acquisition of
wealth and riches open to them was to follow a pattern of partly
expansionist, autonomous growth in which they were forced to
accept a high degree of dependence upon others. In other words,

their concentration upon trade and finance tended to produce a pattern of satellitic economic development. The fortunes of these city states, even when, as did Florence, Milan, and Venice, they developed sizable industries — cloth-finishing in Florence, ship-building in Venice — were dependent upon foreign trade, and hence upon the fortunes of areas beyond their political control. In the case of shipbuilding the dependence is obvious; in the case of Florentine industrial products, the rise of the Calimala guild points to the fact that the real strength of the economy lay in that branch of the cloth industry which was most closely interwoven with foreign trade.

Given the political conditions of the time and the general state of society which made this development of foreign trade possible, the cities build social structures in which the originally autonomous tendencies of growth became more and more controlled by a financial and commercial oligarchy. The satellitic character of the development was therefore made more distinct, since each of the city states became increasingly dependent upon one powerful country or social group outside. Florence tended to become dependent upon the papacy and later upon France, Genoa upon Spain, and Venice, after the fall of Constantinople, upon the Ottoman Empire. At the onset of the sixteenth century we find the top of the social hierarchy occupied by a mercantile and financial aristocracy which is jealous of its monopoly and dependent for its political and economic fortunes upon one, or at best, a limited number of outside powers (12).

With the geographical shifts produced by the discoveries, and the rise of competitors to Italian commercial hegemony in Portugal and the Netherlands and to Italian financial hegemony in upper Germany and France, the task which Italian communities faced was

to further their own development. It would have been important
for northern Italy to give up its dependence on outsiders and to
enter upon a policy of dominant development, to underplay the
tendencies of commercial and financial expansionism and to
stress intrinsic industrial development, and finally to reattain
the degree of autonomy which it had reached in the early Middle
Ages. This course would have required to reallocation of social
and political power in the cities. It did not occur though it was
the only effective means of preventing the gradual economic decline of the region. In other words, given the changed conditions
in which these city states found themselves and which were produced by developments beyond their immediate control, their
further prosperity depended upon a change in the pattern of growth
which they had followed successfully in the past. The very success of the past pattern had entrenched in power a social class
which resisted change and which was successful in its resistance
because it was so powerful.

It would, of course, be wrong to assert that the financial and commercial elite of the Italian cities did not sense that the economic
future of its society lay in a change of the pattern of development.
The senate of Venice introduced a textile industry. Similarly in
Milan steps were taken to foster industrial development. Grand
Duke Ferdinand I of Tuscany undertook a large-scale programme
of agricultural development, which included the reclamation of
the Val di Chiana and the Siennese Maremma. He attracted immigrants — a common mercantilist device — and supported the
textile, especially the silk, industry. But all these steps were
inadequate. The only practical method would have been to follow
a pattern of autonomous rather than induced development. It was
imperative to attract the medium-sized and small bourgeoisie,

to open up for it — as was done in Britain and Holland, and to a lesser extent in France — channels for upward mobility in the social scale and to place a positive valuation on the acquisition of wealth through industrial enterprise. The failure of the Reformation to take hold in Italy was probably a factor which prevented this development. But the control of the financial aristocracy was too complete to permit a loosening of the social order in which greater upward mobility by means other than landholding or financing governments became possible. Evidence for this contention is supplied best by the role of Ferdinand of Tuscany himself. His energetic measures for intrinsic development have been mentioned. But he also set up a government monopoly in the grain trade, he participated in the industrial and banking enterprises stimulated by him, and he was believed by common rumour, at the end of his reign, to have been the richest man of his age.

The answer to the problem of the reasons for the economic decline of northern Italy takes on a surer and more compelling form when we state it in terms of the variables discussed in this paper. To be sure, the factors which have been commonly stressed are not deprived of their validity, but their interrelation is made plainer and more logical. The role of Protestantism, the shift of world commerce to the Atlantic are not seen as independent unrelated events, but as causes and consequences logically bound up with the changing patterns and needs of the economic growth of Italy. And the failure of nerve is not attributed in a naive fashion to the degenerating influence of wealth and luxury, but rather to the structure of society which grew out of one pattern of economic development, but was an impediment to the evolution of another more suited to meet the challenge presented by the changed conditions.

V

I now wish, in conclusion, to show the applicability of our set of variables to a problem of economic development in the contemporary world, in particular the economic problem faced by the five countries of Central America (13), which together have eight million inhabitants, the most populous of them three million. Up to 1840 these countries formed a political unit, but each has followed an independent course since that time. Their economies are similar. They are all exporters of one or two staple agricultural crops. Coffee and bananas make up approximately 85 per cent of the total exports of the region. These countries, which, in terms of per capita incomes, are among the poorest in Latin America, have plans for economic development which were worked out with the help of the World Bank, United States Technical Aid Missions, or the United Nations Technical Cooperation Administration. The United Nations has strongly supported regional economic integration and feeble first steps in the implementation of this policy have been taken.

The problem before these countries is to choose between individual plans pursued independently and joint planning for the development of the whole region. Though it is often asserted that this second alternative would require political unification, it might be achieved merely by economic union administered by regional development boards with real power. We may disregard for the time being the constitutional issue because, in practice, a regional planning board with real powers will be as difficult to achieve as political unification or federation.

The difficulties in the path of effective economic co-operation

favour the alternative that each country follow its own development plans. But in view of the smallness of each country and its
undifferentiated resources, the only possible path to development
is one in which the satellitic character of the relation of each
country to the United States is preserved, and possibly even
strengthened. This is precisely the outcome which these countries wish to avoid. They wish to embark upon a programme of
development which will enable them in the near future to follow
a path of dominant growth.

Moreover, as long as the countries follow independent plans
of development and hence continue to be dependent upon the United
States market for bananas and coffee for their foreign exchange
receipts, they will continue to pursue an intrinsic developmental
policy. Yet in all five countries there are sparsely populated
tropical lowlands into which population could be moved. Apart
from very limited shifts in population, especially in the course
of the opening up of new banana lands, the present and planned
developmental policies — notably in the fields of transportation,
agriculture, and industrialization — do not foreshadow an expansionist pattern of growth. Nor would, under present conditions,
such a policy be of much value. The choice before the countries,
therefore, is either to accept induced satellitic intrinsic development and maintain full economic independence from one another,
or to follow a path of induced, partially expansionist, and ultimately dominant development and enter into a federation or regional economic block.

In a sense the position of the Central American countries today
is analogous to that of Canada before Confederation. Even the incentives for common economic action in Central America are similar to those which prevailed in Canada in 1867. The need for rail-

way-building, for the development of the western provinces, and
for the creation of an internal market for the industries of Ontario,
and the grave financial problems faced by all the colonies were
among the chief economic factors favouring Confederation. The
relation of the colonies to Britain and the United States remained
satellitic in character to some extent after Confederation, but
expansionism became economically possible and profitable. This
pattern ultimately led to an integration of resources under one
government which could, after a period, embark upon a policy
of fostering dominant economic growth and in this way attain higher economic integration of the country coupled with higher real
incomes.

In Central America, also, economic union will mean the extension of railways and other transportation facilities to the lowlands; this in turn may lead to the production of new commodities
to supply growing internal markets; and may further produce an
impetus for domestic industrialization; finally, an economic union
would benefit the countries' finances since it would prevent competitive over-investment in a few lines of industrial production,
such as textiles and cement. Though the countries would remain
satellites to the United States market for some time to come, they
would have a real possibility of entering eventually upon dominant
economic growth.

The procedures applied in these two cases could be extended
also to others. I do not pretend that they will revolutionize our
insights about the conditions of economic progress. But they may
make possible a more fruitful integration of economic and non-
economic variables which together provide an adequate explanation
of the different patterns of economic development that have been
ascertained in the historical experience of the advanced countries

and that are so warmly discussed in the underdeveloped parts of the world.

NOTES TO CHAPTER IV

*This paper was presented at the annual meeting of the Canadian Political Science Association in Toronto, June 1, 1955. I wish to express my gratitude to Professors Richard Hartshorne and Joseph J. Spengler who read and discussed with me an earlier draft. I owe many fruitful suggestions to them. The blunders are all mine.

1. Joseph Schumpeter, Imperialism and Social Classes (New York, 1955), p. 25.

2. Henry Nash Smith, Virgin Land (Cambridge, Mass., 1950), 123 ff., passim.

3. For Italy and Flanders see Jean Lestocquoy, Les Villes de Flandre et d'Italie sous le gouvernement des patriciens (Paris, 1952), passim; for the Hansa towns see Fritz Rörig, Hansische Beiträge zur deutschen Wirtschaftsgeschichte (Breslau, 1928), esp. chaps. I-III and VII; for upper Germany see Jakob Strieder, Zur Genesis des modernen Kapitalismus (2nd ed., Berlin, 1935).

4. The episode reported in the paragraph has been analysed in greater detail by Charles P. Kindleberger in "Group Behavior and International Trade," Journal of Political Economy, Vol. 50, No. 1 (Feb, 1951), pp. 30-46.

5. Friedrich Engels, Socialism: Utopian and Scientific (Chicago, 1902), p. 123.

6. See Martin Bronfenbrenner, "The Appeal of Confiscation in Economic Development," Economic Development and Cultural Change, Vol. 3, No. 3 (April, 1955), pp. 204-9.

7. See Simon Kuznets, "Population, Income and Capital" in Leon H. Dupriez, ed., Economic Progress: Papers and Proceedings of a Round Table Held by the International Economic Association (Louvain, 1955), pp. 43-5.

8. Gregory Grossman, "National Income" in Abram Bergson, ed., Soviet Economic Growth (Evanston, Ill., 1953), pp. 8-10.

9. See Alexander Gerschenkron, "Economic Backwardness in Histori-Perspective" in Bert F. Hoselitz, ed., The Progress of Underdeveloped Areas (Chicago, 1952), p. 10.

10. The points alluded to in this paragraph are discussed in greater length in my essay, "Entrepreneurship and Capital Formation in France and Britain since 1700" in Moses Abramovitz, ed., Capital Formation and Economic Growth, (Princeton, 1955), pp. 297-304.

11. A good discussion along somewhat "traditional" lines of the economic decline of northern Italy is presented by Alfred Doren, <u>Italienische Wirtschaftsgeschichte</u> (Jena, 1934), pp. 675 ff.

12. The discussion in this and the subsequent two paragraphs owes much to the masterly study by Fernand Braudel, <u>La Méditerranée et le monde méditerranéen à l'époque de Philippe II</u> (Paris, 1949), esp. pp. 268 ff., 421 ff., and 549-50.

13. The points raised in this section are discussed in greater length in my article, "Economic Development in Central America," <u>Weltwirtschaftliches Archiv,</u> Vol. 76, No. 2 (June, 1956), pp. 267-308.

5

POPULATION PRESSURE, INDUSTRIALIZATION AND SOCIAL MOBILITY

The rapid growth of population which we witness in many countries of Asia, Africa, and Latin America provoked a large amount of reflection as to the measures which might be taken in order to cope with this development which threatens to worsen average living standards in these countries. In the countries of Asia and the Middle East which already exhibit high population densities in rural areas, the problem of finding employment opportunities for the growing labour force is especially pressing, because fragmentation of land-holdings, and the exploitation of marginal lands sets limits to a further extension of employment in agriculture. The principal solution proposed to find productive employment for the growing labour force is planned industrialization and the past experiences of economically advanced countries have been cited as proof that this development is not merely desirable, but virtually inevitable if living standards are to rise.

I do not wish to dispute the basic thought underlying this analysis, but because of several profound differences in the economic and demographic structure of the densely settled countries of Asia and the Middle East and the countries of Europe at the time they began to industrialize it is desirable to investigage somewhat more

115

fully the probable conditions of industrialization in Asia and to ascertain, if possible, whether the past experience of Western countries can provide a "lesson" for Asia's future. On the surface it appears as if that experience will repeat itself. Sprawling cities, filled with industrial and commercial enterprises have already grown up. Slums, alcoholism, prostitution, hazards to health and personal safety which have been so widely castigated in the cities of nineteenth century Europe by writers inclined towards a pastoral romanticism have been noted in Asian cities also. As in Europe of former days, we find in India, Ceylon, Malaya and elsewhere a developing commercial and managerial middle class, an incipient white-collar and "blue-collar" proletariat, and a gradual transformation of social, economic, and political power from the large landholders to urban capitalists and intellectuals. History appears to repeat itself.

And yet, there are significant differences in the conditions which existed when Europe industrialized and those we find in Asia to-day. Not only can we discover important differences in the "economic ethic," but also in more tangible concrete factors; factors determining the capacity for capital formation and the forms of economic organization. One of the most obvious is the much greater rural density of population in most Asian countries as compared with Western countries to-day, and even at an earlier period. Not many efforts have been made in the past to present adequate comparative statistical data on agricultural densities and agricultural densities have been given little attention in the analysis of economic growth. Yet, some recently published figures by Colin Clark (1) seem to indicate that agricultural densities should be given higher priority, since in general there exists a rather high correlation between agricultural land per agricultural worker and average per capita output. And those countries which fall rather outside the main regression line represent special cases, which have their own special explanations.

Clark's procedure consists in computing for each country, areas of "standard farm land." The entire potentially agricultural area of a country is converted to standard units of land, by multiplying each region by a factor greater than, equal to, or less than unity, depending upon conditions of natural fertility (chiefly climatic conditions) in the given region. Thus, for example, a piece of land on which two crops per year can be grown would be multiplied by the factor 2, and some semi-arid land suitable for sparse pasture only by a factor of 1/100th. Land which with given technology cannot be exploited agriculturally would have a factor of zero. If the amount of standard farm land gained by these procedures is divided by the number of males occupied in agriculture, we obtain an agricultural density figure which is a fairly realistic indication of the relation between the human and the most important non-human factor in agricultural production.

The results obtained by Mr. Clark show that whereas in North America, the large grazing countries of South America and Australia, there are between 0.33 and 1.89 occupied males per square kilometre of standard farm land, the corresponding densities in Western Europe are between 4.27 and 12.4 (2), in Eastern and Southern Europe between 12 and 25, in Japan 17.35, in India 26.8, and in the arid and semi-arid countries of the Near East between 30 and 75. These data all relate to the 1930's, at which time the various countries included in the comparison had very different proportions of their labour force in agriculture. Just as we have found a high correlation between average product and the reciprocal of agricultural density and the proportion of the gainfully employed

population in agriculture. In other words, we cannot tell whether
the high agricultural densities in Asia and Africa are due chiefly
to the greater overall population densities of these countries, or
to the larger proportion of the working populations in agriculture.

In order to obtain some indication of the significance of the
"population obstacle" to economic development in present-day
Asia — as compared with Europe at the early phase of its industrial revolution — I have attempted to compute some data on
agricultural densities in various countries at a period when the
approximate proportion of gainfully employed persons in agriculture was between 55 and 75 per cent. These proportions correspond roughly to those prevailing currently in most underdeveloped
countries of South Asia and the Middle East. The figures are presented in Table V-1. While I was unable to convert data for agricultural land surface into units of standard farm land, as Mr.
Clark has done, I believe that the unrefined figures presented in
Table V-1 are in themselves quite revealing. It goes without saying
that many of the data are based on rather crude estimates. This
is true both of the earlier European data and the current data from
Asia and the Middle East. Thus the figures in the last column of
the table, which indicate the number of hectares of agricultural land
per gainfully occupied male in agriculture or per agricultural household, should be regarded not as precise indications of average farm
land available, but rather as guides to the overall order of magnitude of agricultural land as the disposal of the average cultivator
or farm household in the various countries. It should also be noted
that one of the two main variables presented in the table could not
be held constant. What we wish to compare is agriculturally usable
farm area with the number of farm workers. The former includes
all arable land, gardens, orchards, fallow and permanent pasture.

The latter may be measured either by the number of all persons
(male and female) gainfully employed in agriculture, or only by
males so employed, or by the number of agricultural households.
One can adduce reasons in favour of each of the three measures
(3), but in Table V-1 either occupied males or agricultural households have been used, depending upon what figures were available
or could be computed without too large a margin of error. In the
third column of the Table, the letter M or H, designates which
of the two measures was employed in each case. M stands for
the number of males occupied in agriculture, and H for the number of agricultural households.

The results of this table may be summarized as follows: (1) In
general we find that agricultural densities — whether measured
in terms of occupied males or in terms of households — are roughly
three or more times as high in present-day underdeveloped countries in Asia, as in Europe at a corresponding period of the economic development if we measure economic development by the proportion of the gainfully occupied population or of households in
primary production. (2) In Japan, the one case for which the table
contains figures for two periods at very different stages of economic development, we find that agricultural density has not changed
very much. This means that although the proportion of gainfully
employed persons in agriculture has steadily declined, their absolute number has remained fairly constant. In other words, the
data from Japan indicate that though the country was undergoing
relatively rapid industrialization, it was unable to reduce the
total absolute number of persons in agriculture from what it was
at an early stage of the industrialization process.

But there is a fair deal of additional evidence showing that even
in more advanced countries the absolute number of persons engaged

in agriculture did not decline until a very late stage of industrialization had been reached. Hence the absolute number of active
males in agriculture, increased between 1900 and 1950 in all
European countries except the most highly industrialized ones
of Western and Central Europe. Similarly in Italy which in 1900
had an agricultural density of 3.5 hectares per worker, and in
1950 one of 3.6 per worker, it was estimated that the agricultural
density in 1861 was about 4 hectares per active male in agriculture. Finally an observation of occupational distributions in
various European countries in different census years shows that
the absolute size of the agricultural labour force did not begin to
decline in Britain until the 1870's, in Germany until the 1920's
and in Switzerland until the 1910's. In Norway, the Netherlands,
Austria, Finland, and Portugal the absolute number of occupied
persons in agriculture in 1950 was higher than at the beginning of
the 19th century (4).

Yet we know that during the whole period which preceded the
decline of the agricultural labour force in these countries, economic growth occurred at a rapid rate, in some countries at the most
rapid rate of their recorded history (5). This process of expansion
was accompanied by rapid population growth, and although secondary
and tertiary industries expanded with sufficient rapidity to absorb
the increasing numbers of entrants to the labour force, their expansion was not rapid enough to relieve agricultural density in
any noticeable degree.

Yet in European countries in which agricultural density in the
early stages of industrialization was lower than currently in Asia,
the rate of expansion of non-agricultural employment opportunities
was lower than would have to be the case in Asia if the entire additional population is to be absorbed in secondary and tertiary industries.

Table V-1. Density of agricultural settlement in countries with more than half the active labour force in agriculture

(1) Country	(2) Year	(3) M or H	(4) Agricultural land in 1000 ha.	(5) No. of M or H in 1000	(6) % of M or H in total such units	(7) Ha. per Ha. per M or H
Ceylon (a) ..	1954/55	M	1,508	1,032	51	1.46
India (b)	1954/55	H	146,377	71,100	68	2.06
Malaya (a) ..	1954/55	M	2,219	889	61	2.50
Pakistan (a).	1954/55	M	24,297	16,096	76	1.51
Phillipines (a)	1954/55	M	5,727	2,826	64	2.03
Thailand (a).	1954/55	M	4,750	3,823	82	1.24
Taiwan (b) ..	1953	H	873	725	56	1.20
Egypt (a)....	1954/55	M	2,451	3,656	63	0.67
Japan (a) ...	1955	M	6,451	9,000	37	0.72
Japan (c)....	1886	H	5,665	5,518	71	1.03
Finland (d)..	1900	M	2,849	465	69	6.74
Portugal (d).	1900	M	4,860	1,147	61	4.24
Spain (d)....	1900	M	30,119	4,300	67	7.00
Italy (d)	1901	M	22,260	6,390	59	3.48
Sweden (e) ..	1870	H	4,534	672	72	6.75
Denmark (f).	1861	M	2,444	281	53	8.70
Bavaria (g)..	1840	H	4,201	606	63	6.93
Prussia (g)..	1858	H	15,506	1,658	46	9.35
France (h) ..	1851	M	32,831	6,600	53	4.97
England and Wales (i) ..	1688	H	9,510	900	70	10.57

Footnotes refer to sources —
a. International Labour Office, Yearbook of Labour Statistics 1956, Geneva, 1956 Table 4 and Food and Agriculture Organization, Yearbook of Food and Agricultural Statistics, 1954, Part I, Rome 1955, Table I.

b. Food and Agriculture Organization, Documentation Prepared for the Center on Land Problems in Asia and the Far East held in Bangkok, Thailand, 22 Nov. — 11 December, 1954. Rome, 1955.

c. Karl Rathgen, Japan's Volkswirtschaft und Staatshaushalt, Leipzig, 1891, pp. 750-3.

d. Folke Dovring, Land and Labour in Europe 1900-1950, The Hague, 1953, Table 3, pp. 66-67, and Appendix to Table 3, pp. 379 ff.

e. G. A. Montgomery, The Rise of Modern Industry in Sweden, London, 1939, pp. 61; Elis Sidenblath, Schweden, Statistische Mitteilungen, Stockholm, 1873, p. 43; and Statistiska Central-Bryans, Befolknings-Statistik for ar 1870, Stockholm, 1873, pp. xv-xvi.

f. Dovring, op. cit., p. 383, and Denmark, Statens Statistiske Bureau, Befolknings-forholdene i Danmark i det 19. aarhundrede, (Statistisk Tabelvaerk, 5th Series, Lit. A no. 5), Kopenhagen, 1905, passim.

g. Georg v. Viehbahn, Statistik des zollvereinten und nordlichen Deutschlands, vol. II, Berlin, 1862, pp. 274-276, 540-546, 607.

h. "Evolution de la population active en France depuis 100 ans," Etudes et Conjoncture VII, no. 3 (Mar-June 1953) p. 235, France, Bureau de la Statistique Générale, Statistique de la France, 2nd ser., vol. II, Paris 1855, pp. 6-7.

i. Gregory King, "Natural and Political Observations and Conclusions upon the State and Condition of England," in Two Tracts, ed. by G. E. Barnett, Baltimore, 1936, pp. 20 ff.

Hence, we have little reason to expect that Asian countries can hope to see within the next decades a decline in the absolute number of persons dependent upon agriculture for their livelihood.

To some extent pressures upon the agriculture of industrializing European countries were relieved by emigration, and for the rest industrialization absorbed the growing labour force. But in Asia potentialities of emigration are strictly limited and, given the low level of income and the very considerable density of rural population, agricultural population pressure is likely to be greater in future years. How tenacious this stability of agricultural population may be is expressed by Professor Yuzo Morita when he says that

> "the proportion of agricultural population has gradually shrunk since the Meiji Era, but it also is true... that there has been no substantial change in the absolute scale of the agricultural industry in Japan. The agricultural population numbered... 1e million early in the Meiji Era. This figure did not show appreciable increase thereafter, and the overall scale of Japanese agriculture had been indicated for the several decades until the beginning of the Pacific War by the three almost always constant figures: households engaged in agriculture, 5.5 millions, agricultural labour force, 14 millions, and total cultivated land 6 million cho" (6).

Since rates of population increase show a tendency to remain high in most Asian countries, it is likely that great pressures for the extension of the agricultural area will remain, even if abundant employment opportunities should occur in secondary and tertiary production. In response to this pressure, efforts will be undertaken to increase the effective land area in agriculture. Apart from the use of higher-yielding crops, insecticides and other plant preservatives which result in increased output per unit of land area, there are two ways in which the effective area under agriculture may be increased. One is the spatial expansion of agricultural land by land reclamation, drainage, irrigation, the construction of sea walls, or terracing, and the other is by increasing the capacity of a given area to bear more than one crop per year, through the application of fertilizers, water, and appropriate rotation of crops. If the average farm household in an underdeveloped country tills three acres to-day, it may have six acres to-morrow if either the total agricultural surface is doubled, or if on its three acres it can grow two crops annually instead of one. Which of these two alternatives will be preferable depends upon relative cost conditions in each country. In Japan, where the addition to the existing agriculturally usable area was associated with very high costs, the application of fertilizers, the rotation of crops, and irrigation were used so as to produce two or, in some cases, even three crops on the same piece of land. In parts of Burma, Thailand, Indonesia, and Malaya, where additional land can be put to agricultural use with relatively little additional capital outlay, the extension of the surface under agriculture may be more advisable. But, whichever pattern of development prevails in the short run, it may be assumed, as a general rule, that as land settlement extends further and further, the marginal cost of adding to agricultural land will increase so that at some point land reclamation "in depth," rather than "in width" will tend to become of increasing significance (7).

But whichever pattern is chosen, it is unlikely that, given the costs of land reclamation, the average size of agricultural holding will increase very much, if at all. Present population densities in the countryside are too great and the mobilization of capital for non-agricultural production not rapid enough to relieve pressure on land within the foreseeable future. Hence, in the absence of major technological innovations in agriculture, we may anticipate that the countries stretching from the arid Middle Eastern region across southern and south eastern Asia will be characterized in the future by small-scale labour intensive agriculture, and that even as the application of capital to agriculture expands, it will consist chiefly in fertilizers, water, and such other forms of capital which will enhance the intensity of exploitation of a small plot rather than a more extensive method of farming which is increasingly characteristic of the West. The Asian style of agriculture, however, is distinguished chiefly from the western style in that the maximization of return per unit of land input rather than per unit of labour input is sought. As a consequence, as long as pressure on land persists, returns to labour in Asian agriculture will not reach levels commensurate with those reached in European or American agriculture. But this means, at the same time, that the differential between returns in agriculture and industry will be greater in Asia than in Europe. For example, in 1950-51 income per occupied person in primary industry amounted in Japan only to 38 per cent of income in secondary and tertiary industry, whereas in Britain the corresponding figure was 110 per cent, in the United States, 55 per cent, in Western Germany, 48 per cent, and in Italy 54 per cent (8).

This development in Asian agriculture is contingent upon the absorption of rural "surplus" population in secondary and tertiary industries. This requires the creation of employment opportunities in manufacturing, trade, and service industries. Now a widely held view of this process conceives it as consisting in the establishment of large plants using large-scale machinery, and absorbing vast amounts of fixed capital. This is a somewhat romantic view of the industrialization process, which, in fact, has consisted in all countries not merely in the establishment of large-scale plants, but the

simultaneous growth of many small and even minute enterprises.
This pattern emerges especially in countries with an old culture
in which handicrafts and similar trades have been long developed
and in which there exist strong "industrial" traditions already.
This simultaneous development of large-scale and small-scale
industry has taken place in all European countries which escaped
the fetters of economic backwardness, and it can be observed
clearly in Japan. In many countries of South Asia arguments in
favour of the potential contribution to economic development which
small-scale industry can make have been expressed, and in recent
years interest in fostering small-scale and "cottage" industries has
been widespread. The case for the maintenance of cottage and
small-scale industries in capital-poor countries with a dense rural
population may be supported from an economic viewpoint in the
manner of Professor W. Arthur Lewis (9). His major arguments
are that in countries which have surplus labour, capital can, in
the early stages of growth, be put to better advantage by applying
it to the construction of public utilities, and those industrial establishments in which for technological reasons large-scale production has the greatest advantage, than to a number of consumer
goods industries in which the small-scale firm is comparatively
less disadvantaged; that in an agricultural situation in which persons are partly underemployed, either for most of the year or
during part of the year, cottage industries may supply part-time
employment for this less than fully employed population; and,
finally, that small-scale and cottage industries have the advantage
of economizing two factors which are notoriously scarce in underdeveloped countries, capital and managerial skill.

In the last report all these arguments may be reduced to the
proposition that small-scale industries are suited for developing

countries with dense populations because they require a composition
of productive factors in which those which are relatively abundant
in such countries are substituted for those relatively scarce. In
more concrete terms, simple or relatively little skilled labour
which is available in abundance is employed in large amounts and
capital and managerial services, which are scarce, are used
sparingly. Although these ratios are accurate if looked at from
the viewpoint of factor inputs, it is doubtful whether small-scale
and cottage industries are so economical from the viewpoint of
total output. To be sure, they employ more labour relative to
capital and entrepreneurial services than large-scale industry.
But there seems to be good evidence also that they are more costly
in terms of capital then large-scale industry, i. e., a given output is produced using more labour and more capital by small-scale
industry than by large-scale industry. Evidence for this fact is
not too conclusive, but on the basis of some data presented by Mr.
V. V. Bhatt, this appears to be the case in India; and Bhatt's
findings are supported by careful studies by D. K. Malhotra and
K. N. Raj on the economics of Indian textile production using different technologies (10).

Bhatt compares small-scale, medium-scale, and large-scale
plants in India in ten industries, all of them other than textiles.
A small-scale and a large-scale plant is defined somewhat differently depending upon the industry, but in most cases small-
scale plants have less than 250 workers and most large-scale
plants have more than 500 workers. In all ten cases the ratio of
the net value of plant and equipment to the annual gross value of
output is higher in small-scale plants than in large-scale plants;
in some cases the difference is not very large, but in four cases
capital costs in small-scale plants are roughly three times as high

as in large-scale plants, and in one case, the production of matches, capital costs in small-scale industry are about twelve times those of large-scale industry. Malhotra's findings are parallel. He computes the investment required to produce an output of 300 million yards of cloth, and finds that by using composite mills this cost would amount to Rs. 260.0 million, by using power looms, Rs. 307.5 million, by using handlooms with mill-spun yarn, the cost would be Rs. 341.8 million, and by using handlooms with ambar yarn, the cost would be Rs. 487.9 million. If we contrast the two most likely alternatives, i.e., that between a composite mill and handlooms using mill-spun yarn, we find that the cottage industry requires a capital investment 31 per cent greater than the large-scale plant alternative.

It is true that Bhatt's results are reached by taking account of existing technologies in large-scale and small-scale industry, and it might be argued that existing methods in small-scale and cottage industries are notoriously backward and inefficient. But Malhotra's data are presumably based on modern up-to-date technologies in small-scale industry as well as large-scale industry, and as we have seen, he also arrives at a higher capital cost for a given output if this output is produced by a small weaver than if it is produced in mills. Moreover, it might be argued that Malhotra has estimated only the capital costs in the narrow sense, i.e., those involved in the actual production of the cloth and has left out of consideration accessory capital costs, such as those for warehousing and distributing the raw material and the finished product, and others. If these were included in the estimate the small-scale alternative would emerge as requiring a differential in capital costs even larger than 31 per cent.

This leads to the further consideration that a greater degree of dispersal of industry, i.e., its development in small plants located in many small and medium sized population centres tends to increase the cost of social overhead installations, and to press, in this manner, more heavily upon capital requirements for the development process. Thus the main reason in favour of small-scale and cottage industries is the argument that they are labour intensive and likely to provide immediate employment for persons presently totally unemployed or under-employed.

The employment argument is, of course, a strong one in countries with dense rural populations, and is likely to have sufficient force to direct the attention of policy makers to foster and protect small-scale and cottage industries, even though from a purely long-run economic viewpoint, they may be inefficient and costly. Moreover, in countries in which sufficient scope is allowed for private investment in industry, a substantial amount of capital may be available only in small dribbles, which, owing to the absence of an effective money market can be mobilized only in the form of small and medium-scale enterprises, rather than in its joint application as equity capital in large-scale plants. Hence the absence of a well developed capital market, and the lack of familiarity with corporate forms of enterprise, may, for practical reasons, make possible investment of a proportion of locally available private capital only in small dispersed plants rather than in large capital-intensive plants.

Finally, we may expect small-scale dispersed industries to develop because of the fragmentation of markets in underdeveloped countries. Although the construction of transport and communication facilities tends to enlarge markets and ultimately creates a national market for most commodities, these facilities are too sparse as yet in most underdeveloped countries, and their use often too costly for many ordinary commodities which form the utensils of daily life of the poorer classes. There are differences in tastes and local customs, and there exist precisely because of the absence of a well-functioning transport system, opportunities of exploiting local monopoly situations, which may make the establishment of small industrial plants in many places attractive.

Now, as we have seen, the main economic disadvantage of small-scale industry is its lower all-round productivity. As concerns the lower productivity of capital, as compared with larger plants, technological innovations might be found at least in some branches of production, which would eradicate or minimize this disadvantage of small-scale industry. But as far as the lower productivity of labour is concerned, its overall impact will be the acceptance of lower wages by cottage and small-scale industrial workers. Again the experience of Japan is instructive in this field. In Table V-2, wages and hours worked in large and small-scale plants are compared with one another, and from this comparison it appears that monthly wages in the first half of 1955 in Japanese small-scale industry (i.e., plants with fewer than 100 workers) were only roughly three-fifths of wages in large-scale plants (i.e., with more than 500 workers). This difference is not due to the fact that small-scale plants employ primarily part-time workers, for the number of hours worked in small-scale plants was approximately 7 per cent more than in large-scale plants, so that differences in hourly wages amounted to 54 percentage points between plants of the two size classes. These are data taken from a country in which technological change has already progressed far, and in which many technical and organizational innovations have been introduced also in small-scale industry. It is possible, of course, that the lower wages in smaller plants are due, in part,

Table V-2. Wages and Hours in Large and Small-Scale Manufacturing Industry in Japan, January-July, 1955.

Size of Firm	Monthly wage in Yen	No. of hours per month	Wage per hour in Yen	in %
30-99 workers	11,546	201.8	57.22	75.7
100-499 workers.....	14,361	196.4	73.12	96.8
more than 500 workers	18,357	187.6	97.85	129.5
Average	14,755	195.3	75.55	100.0

Source: Asia Kyokai, The Smaller Industries in Japan, (Tokyo,
1957), pp. 100-101.

to the monopolistic exploitation of smaller firms by larger firms,
but this factor alone could not be made accountable for such a large
differential, and the difference must ultimately be explained by
differences in the productivity of labour.

The continued presence, and, indeed, the spread into new
productive fields of small-scale industries must be explained by
the abundance of new entrants into the labour force, who cannot
find further employment in agriculture because there the limits
of expansion have been reached, and who cannot find employment
in large-scale industry, because the growth of population occurs
at a faster rate than investment which would absorb all new entrants
to the labour force in modern highly productive industrial or tertiary employment. It is true that in Japan the development of
small-scale industry was helped by the existence of traditional
forms of social interdependence inherited from an earlier "feudalistic" system (11). This system provided for the more rational
supply of raw materials and sale of finished products of small
firms, it made available credit on relatively adequate terms and
established working routines which ensured the permanence of
operations. But at the same time, the continued existence of small-

scale industry around the fringes of large-scale plants, maintained a persistent pattern of earning differentials in industry. Many of the small industries are located in cities, or suburban areas not far removed from places in which large-scale highly productive plants operate. This means, however, that there are in existence — and have been in existence in Japan for some time — two non-agricultural labour forces. Both are essentially urban, both employ relatively modern machinery, both are decidedly removed from agricultural production. But the earnings of one group are substantially lower than those of the other, and this differential in wages, which amounts to somewhere between one-third and two-fifths, appears to have persisted in spite of the modernization and rationalization of small-scale production. In fact the income pattern of workers in smaller industries resembles in magnitude the incomes of farmers, whereas the incomes of industrial workers in large-scale plants are visibly higher.

Now differentials between earnings in agriculture and industry are, as we have seen, not uncommon, and may be found in most advanced countries also. It is also agreed that there are in all countries differentials in industrial wages. But in most cases these wage differentials are due to different skill levels required in different industries, to regional differences in wage patterns, or to differences in the effectiveness of trade union activity in different branches of production. In Japan, where substantial differences exist between large-scale and small-scale industry, part of the explanation may be provided by the more extensive action of trade unions in larger plants. Yet the overall pattern of earnings in Japanese industry does not appear to have changed much as a consequence of changes in the strength and organization efficiency of trade unions (12). And for the last thirty years at least, and probably ever since the restoration of the Meiji emperor, Japanese industry has been divided into two branches; and with the development of technology the economic and productivity differences between them have become wider rather than narrower.

These developments appear to be a consequence of the serious population pressure which existed in Japan at the beginning of its industrialization process, and of the inability to raise capital in large enough amounts to set up industrial units of large size throughout all fields of secondary and tertiary production. Their consequence has been the persistence of two distinct bodies of wage earners with widely different living standards. Since population pressure, scarcity of capital, and the lack of an adequately functioning money market are characteristics also of other countries in Asia, we may expect that their industrialization process will follow lines somewhat similar to those of Japan, and that there also, workers in industries with different degrees of productivity and hence on very different earning levels will appear.

If these workers have access to the same labour market, i.e., if differences in earnings are found in the same community, and if workers with access to jobs paying different wages are not distinguished by skill level or place of residence, the persistence of such differentials in earnings can only be maintained if mechanisms are developed which prevent widespread mobility of labour. Such mechanisms, may be formal, i.e., laws may be instituted which prevent persons from moving freely from a low-wage to a higher-wage job, or they may be informal. In countries with totalitarian political organizations, such mechanisms are usually formal. In Japan, mechanisms preventing the free mobility of labour have, on the whole, been informal. It is this tie-in between a person and his job to which Japanese economists sometimes refer, when they talk of "feudalistic survivals" in the Japanese economy.

The social structure of a modern industrial society has been described as presenting universalist, achievement-oriented norms in the assignment of economic roles (13). In a recent study of social conditions in Japanese industrial plants, these relationships have been found to be present only to a very limited degree, and to be contradicted by many actual practices affecting hiring and job continuity. Workers who are hired in a large plant have a good expectation to be kept for a lifetime in their employment with this plant, or at least some other plant of the same firm. Hiring practices, therefore, rely to a large degree not on the technical capacity of workers to perform the tasks they will be asked to do, but rather on personal characteristics of the prospective worker, his affiliation with others in the factory, and his family background and other "ascription" characteristics. The relationships established between managements and workers in Japanese factories are closer and more paternalistic than in corresponding firms in Western Europe or the United States, and the services rendered by, and expected from, an employer by far exceed those normally prevalent in advanced industrial countries (14). This close relationship between employer and employee even in some of the largest Japanese firms is rightly recognized as an analogue to a parent-child relationship, which, given Japanese cultural traditions also implied a hierarchical relationship, with a distribution of authority and responsibility substantially different from those prevailing in a typical universalistic-achievement oriented social structure (15).

It appears that the underlying reason for the transference of these socio-structural relations to modern industry, and above all, for the persistence they have shown in this area where they "don't belong by rights," is their function as an impediment on the free mobility of labour. We find, therefore, in Japan a genuine instance of non-competing groups. But whereas the absence of competition between groups of the labour force in Cairnes's classical statement of this phenomenon is based on differences in skill or education of different sections of the working population (16), the lack of competition in Japan is brought about by informal impediments to the free mobility of workers which are ultimately founded in the existing social structure.

Now the argument which has been developed in this paper is that certain tendencies in industrial structure which have developed historically in Japan are likely to produce analogues in other Asian societies in which rural population densities at the beginning of the industrialization process are high, and in which because of the need to provide employment for rural unemployed or under-employed persons and the fragmentation of capital, scattered small-scale industries are likely to develop. These countries, like Japan, already possess, and are likely to continue to possess, a labour force outside of agriculture which, in consequence of its employment in plants of small or minute size, it endowed with low productivity and hence receives lower than average wages. In the absence of totalitarian controls, it is likely that in these countries also certain informal institutions impeding the free mobility of labour, from small to large industry, will be instituted. Clearly the particular pattern which has arisen in Japan cannot be repeated since it is closely tied to survivals of Japan's pre-industrial social structure. But in a country like India, for example, there are other survivals of socio-structural arrangements, foremost the caste system, which are eminently adaptable to prevent a high degree of social mobility.

This leads us to consider a final point, i. e. , the impact of socio-structural survivals and traditions upon the form of industrialization. In the preceding paragraphs these survivals appeared as dependent variables, i. e. , the impression was created that demographic and economic conditions made their operation imperative, or at least desirable. But one should not forget that these survivals and traditions are, in reality, independent variables. Although old forms of social structures undergo change as a society alters its economic organization, they do not disappear wholesale. In other words the particular pattern of industrialization observable in Japan is not merely an outflow of the demographic and economic conditions prevailing there since the restoration of the Meiji emperor, but also a result of the tenacity of the oyako (father-son) pattern and the rigorous system of hierarchical relations in Japanese social organization inherited from the Tokugawa period. Similarly, it may be expected that, in spite of the exorcism of caste and similar manifestations of "communalism" in India for political reasons, informal social relationships, ultimately derived from the caste system, will survive and impinge upon the pattern of industrial development. Unfortunately we have too few valid empirical studies as yet which indicate the potential impact of patterns of social relations in different Asian countries upon the industrialization process there. But it appears that the ultimate forms, and even the capacity to industrialize will be a result not only of demographic factors and capital supply, but also of the adaptability of existing formal and informal social relations to a new more "rationalized" and technologically more efficient economy.

NOTES TO CHAPTER V

1. Colin Clark, The Conditions of Economic Progress, 2nd revised ed. (London, 1951), Folding Table between pp. 200-201.

2. Belgium and the Netherlands, with densities of 17.9 and 17.0 are exceptions, but it need hardly be pointed out that these highly urbanized countries which maintain an extensive foreign trade in agricultural products engage in a specialized highly labour-intensive agriculture producing such high-value goods as dairy products, meats, vegetables, and fruit.

3. A discussion of the relative merits of these measures may be found in Folke Dovring, Land and Labour in Europe 1900-1950 (The Hague, 1953), pp. 61 ff.

4. Dovring, op. cit., pp. 66 ff, and p. 386; Cf. also "Quelques aspects de l'évolution des populations actives dans les pays d'Europe occidentale," Etudes et Conjoncture, Vol. 9, No. 11 (November 1954), pp. 990-991.

5. See Simon Kuznets, "Quantitative Aspects of the Economic Growth of Nations," Economic Development and Cultural Change, Vol. V, No. I (October, 1956), Tables 2 and 9, (pp. 13 and 38-40).

6. (Yuzo Morita,) Facts about the Population of Japan (Population Problems Series no. 14) (Tokyo, 1956), pp. 20-21, cf. also Table 6 pp. 49-50.

7. It goes without saying that the multiplication of annual crops is possible only in countries and regions of countries with suitable climates, i.e., in which tropical or sub-tropical conditions prevail. But since we are here concerned chiefly with countries of Asia and Africa we may assume that large areas now under cultivation could carry two or even more crops per year if the necessary fertilizer and water could be made available.

8. Morita, op. cit., p. 19.

9. See W. Arthur Lewis, The Theory of Economic Growth, (London, 1955), pp. 136-141.

10. See V. V. Bhatt, "Capital-Output Ratios of Certain Industries: A Comparative Study of Certain Countries," Review of Economics and Statistics, Vol. XXXVI, No. 3 (Aug. 1954), pp. 309-319, esp. Table 13 on p. 317, and K. N. Raj, "Small-Scale Industries: Problem of Technological Change," The Economic Weekly, Vol. 8, No. 15 (April 14, 1956), pp. 438-38.

11. For an excellent description of socio-economic relations of Japanese small-scale industry, see John Pelzel, "The Small Industrialist in Japan," Explorations in Entrepreneurial History, Vol. 7, No. 2 (December, 1954), pp. 79-93.

12. See Tokutaro Yamanaka, "The Nature of Small Industries: A Survey of the Economic Interpretation in Japan," Annals of the Hitotsubashi Academy, Vol. 4, No. 1 (October, 1953), pp. 1-14. See also Table 15 on page 202 of William W. Lockwood, The Economic Development of Japan, (Princeton, 1954), and compare the data on employment and output given in this table with the data cited in this essay.

13. See Marion J. Levy, Jr., "Some Sources of the Vulnerability of the Structures of Relatively Non-industrialized Societies to those of Highly Industrialized Societies," in Bert F. Hoselitz, Ed., The Progress of Underdeveloped Areas (Chicago, 1952), pp. 113-125. See also Chapter II, above.

14. This very sketchy description of Japanese conditions is taken from James C. Abegglen, The Japanese Factory (Glencoe, Ill., 1958). Although Dr. Abegglen provides carefully documented field surveys, the distinctions cited in the text become apparent even to any relatively casual observer of Japanese industrial relations.

Other aspects of this employer-employee relationship which differs widely from those characteristic of Western industrial countries are the payment of subsidies to striking workers, the existence of widespread private retirement plans for discharged workers, and the provision of large and varied "fringe-benefits," such as free excursions, free medical advice and treatment, subsidized housing and food distribution, loans to workers, and other manifest expressions of employers' paternalism. Cf. Suichi Harada, Labour Conditions in Japan (New York, 1928), pp. 226-239; also E. A. Heber, Japanische Industriearbeit, (Zurich, 1912), p. 270.

15. On the primary characteristics of Japanese social structure and the importance of kinship-like relations associated with rigorous hierarchical relations see Jean Stoetzel, Without the Chrysanthemum and and the Sword: A Study of the Attitudes of Youth in Post-war Japan (New York, 1955), pp. 56-57.

16. Cf. J. E. Cairnes, Some Leading Principles of Political Economy Newly Expounded (New York, 1875), pp. 66-67.

6

ENTREPRENEURSHIP AND ECONOMIC GROWTH

In the 175 years since the appearance of Adam Smith's Wealth of Nations, the attention paid by economists to the problems of economic progress has undergone a full cycle. The classical economists dealt primarily with two interrelated problems: the nature of economic advance and the changing distribution of income. As Professor Harrod has recently shown, the bare bones of Ricardo's as well as Malthus' contributions to economic theory consist of an analysis of a dynamic economy, the chief characteristics of which are the effects of capital accumulation and the growth of population (1). The last classical writer who placed these topics in the center of his economic theorizing was Karl Marx.

With the advent of the marginal utility school, the analysis of conditions of economic equilibrium was placed in the center of interest, and although problems of economic development were not completely disregarded they receded into the background. With the appearance of Schumpeter's Theory of Economic Development, interest in "dynamics" was awakened again, and in the last few decades a series of valuable contributions have been made to various theoretical aspects of economic growth (2).

But, with the exception of Schumpeter, economists have stressed only those problems of economic relations in advanced countries, to the examination of which general economic theory was most closely attuned. In the course of applying economic analysis to the problems of underdeveloped countries, most attention was thus paid to the monetary-fiscal aspects of economic growth and the non-human factors of production involved in this process. I propose in this paper to direct my attention chiefly to a problem which so far has received only scanty attention by economists, the role of human resources in the process of economic advancement of underdeveloped areas.

This topic has formidable proportions and cannot be treated in full within the framework of this paper. I shall confine my remarks, therefore, to a specialized point, the place of entrepreneurship in economic development, and hope to show, at least by implication, some of the more general problems arising in a consideration of the role played by human factors of production in the process of economic development (3).

I

Although economists have been concerned for 150 years with describing the role of business leaders in the economy, there does not exist full agreement as to what particular kind of behavior is typical of the entrepreneur. A study of economists' opinions on entrepreneurship leads to strange and sometimes contradictory results. Some writers have identified entrepreneurship with the function of uncertainty-bearing, others with the co-ordination of productive resources, others with the introduction of innovations, and still others with the provision of capital. It is probably true

that at different times and under different institutional conditions each of these aspects may have constituted the primary,
or at least socially most significant function, of entrepreneurs,
and this function was then selected as typical and regarded as the
unique contribution of entrepreneurs in the process of production.
In a recent article, Professor Fritz Redlich has attempted to
bring some order into this chaos of definitions and descriptions,
and, although I do not propose to follow his analysis entirely, his
categories are a useful starting point for the examination of entrepreneurship in underdeveloped countries (4).

Professor Redlich starts with a tripartite division of the entrepreneurial function into capitalist, i.e., supplier of funds and
other non-human resources for the enterprise, manager, i.e.,
supervisor and co-ordinator of productive activities, and entrepreneur in the narrow sense of the term, i.e., planner, innovator,
ultimate decision-maker in a productive enterprise. These
functions can be conceptually separated, although they may be
performed by one and the same person and, on a level of relatively
low economic development, often are performed by one man. Here
is an instance in which the small size of the average business unit,
as well as the low degree of specialization on the level of business
leadership, is a mark of the low level of overall economic development. In the modern corporation, on the other hand, the functions
of capitalist, entrepreneur, and manager are, as a rule, performed
by different individuals, and, indeed, the managerial function is
often distributed among several specialists, such as sales manager,
personnel manager, purchasing manager, and others.

Let us now examine the three major entrepreneurial functions
more closely. The supply of capital is an indispensable feature of
economic development. However, the importance of accumulating

large quantities of capital is sometimes overstressed. In many
instances, new productive enterprises can be started with relatively little capital. Under conditions of economic backwardness,
a small structure, barely larger than an artisan's shop, may constitute a useful beginning of industrial operations. Economic
development, if it is to penetrate widely and deeply into the customary productive processes of a society, does not consist necessarily in the wholesale transfer of the most modern, large-
scale equipment, but rather in the establishment of many de-
centralized plants, making use wherever possible of traditional
manual skills and producing objects or services which can be
easily integrated into the native patterns of economic activities.
Such establishments may be on a minute scale and hence would
require relatively little capital (5).

There exist two chief sources of domestic capital in underdeveloped countries. The most important is probably the government which can raise the needed funds by taxation, or domestic
and foreign borrowing. A second source of native capital is the
existence, in almost all underdeveloped countries, of a class of
local merchants, traders, money lenders, and people with inherited wealth (chiefly landowners). Unlike the peasants, and
perhaps artisans in these countries who largely still adhere to
traditional ideologies, the members of the moneyed classes are
motivated in their economic activities by conceptions similar to
those of their counterparts in the advanced countries. Native
traders and money lenders are fully imbued with the "drive to
amass wealth." They often are engaged in very risky enterprises;
they gamble on long odds; they are sharp bargainers and clearly
intent on exploiting any economic situation to their fullest advantage.

Bearing in mind these two major sources of funds for development we may envisage two types of enterprise becoming possible in underdeveloped countries: the publicly owned, often large-scale and complex enterprise, where entrepreneurial functions are performed by officials of the government and where, owing to the size of the enterprise, the various special entrepreneurial functions are divided among a number of men, and the small private firm, run by an aggressive, venturesome individual who is little distinguished from the capitalist-entrepreneur envisaged by the classical writers on political economy; in short, an individual who may be regarded as the prototype of economic man.

The underdeveloped countries are thus in a situation in which the men playing the leading role in guiding economic development will be either of the manager type of the entrepreneur type in Redlich's terminology. Given a level of economic advancement, it will depend on political decisions, as well as the sources of capital for investment, which of the two forms of business leadership will prevail. If economic development is subjected to rigorous government control, or even if the public sector of the economy is large, the managers are likely to predominate and to impress characteristics of managerial activity on the ideas and practices of entrepreneurship in the developing country. On the other hand, if public enterprises remain rigidly confined to a limited set of industries and are elsewhere kept in the background and if sufficient private capital is forthcoming, a climate of genuine entrepreneurship, such as was present in Western Europe during most of the nineteenth century, may predominate.

In view of these alternatives of industrial organization facing underdeveloped countries, it is important to ask what are the differences between managerial and entrepreneurial functions and

attitudes, and if a significant difference can be found, what are the
factors that tend to facilitate or impede genuine entrepreneurship
from evolving.

The differences between managerial activity and entrepreneurship are considerable. This fact is often overlooked because in
the western world, and notably in countries in which free enterprise capitalism has found vigorous advocates, the assumption is
made that the personnel guiding a corporation forms the collective
equivalent of the individual entrepreneur of early capitalism. From
the standpoint of the economic theory of the firm this procedure has
merit, but if the role of business leaders is examined in a wider
social context, and especially if the role of various business leaders
is related to the special skills and personality traits they exhibit,
we must stress the differences rather than the similarities between
the actions performed by the men at the head of enterprises of different scale.

The distinction between managerial and entrepreneurial activity
goes back to the typology of capitalist behavior, which was first
presented by Werner Sombart. Although Sombart stated this typology
already in 1912, in his Quintessence of Capitalism, he expressed it
perhaps most clearly and succinctly in a speech, delivered in 1932.
Sombart said there:

> The economic ethic peculiar to capitalism is customarily
> designated as "spirit of capitalism." During the last decades
> this spirit has undergone quite substantial changes which
> are apt to alter its essence. This essence lay in the tension
> between rationalism and irrationalism, between calculation
> and speculation, between the bourgeois spirit and the robber
> spirit, between prudence and venturesomeness. But this
> tension has decreased. The rational factor has experienced
> a strong impetus and even a rationalization of entrepreneur-
> ship has taken place, so to speak. We can pursue this change
> in detail. We see how the importance of specific entrepreneur-
> ial activity, of intuition, of a "sixth sense" diminishes. The

number of knowable, predictable circumstances constantly
increases and the inclination of business leaders grows to
base their enterprises on a foundation of knowledge. Enterprises thus attain the character of administrations, their
leaders, the character of bureaucrats, and the gigantic
size of the apparatus contributes to this development (6).

This passage clearly indicates the distinction between the entrepreneur and the manager, but it represents them not merely as performing a different functional role in the economy but also as being
differently motivated and possibly as carriers of particular personality types. In order to examine the form of business leadership in underdeveloped countries, attention to these differences in
motivation and character structure must be paid.

Although studies of the role and personality of managers in advanced countries exist, even though not in too great abundance, it is
questionable how much of this information can be applied to underdeveloped countries. It would seem that the evidence reported from
Soviet Russia has more bearing on our problem. There exists an
excellent study on management in Soviet State-controlled enterprises,
which permits us to derive a few pertinent generalizations (7). The
description of managers in this book is based partly on the study of
real persons and partly on the way in which Soviet managers are
depicted in Soviet literature. The description of plant managers in
Russian industry presented in this work reveals that they are men
whose chief training is in some field of engineering. They regard
the objects as well as the human beings which they command as a
mass of materiel which is to be used to achieve a given end. They
are hardworking, rigid, determined. They ride roughshod over
obstacles; they drive their workers often to exhaustion. They seem
to be human machines and to regard the men who are under them as
machines. They have no regard for human feelings and emotions,
they are devoted to performing a job and all efforts are strained to

achieve this end regardless of the cost in human lives and satis-
faction (8).

This picture is perhaps somewhat overdrawn, but what is important for our purpose is that the typical manager in a Russian
industrial plant is an individual who has a minimum of independent
creative ability, but who is a rigorous executor of other men's
plans. He does not have originality but persistence and devotion
to a task. He is pitiless but just in that he drives himself as hard
as others. And although the family background and the social-structural characteristics of Russian managers have changed drastically
in the last twenty-five years, the personality types have not.

This description is by no means designed to provide a portrait
of the typical bureaucrat in advanced countries. The managerial
personnel of public or private administration in advanced countries,
although possibly exhibiting certain similar traits, is not composed
of individuals whose behavior is identical with that of the heads of
Russian plants. In part the ruthless efficiency with which these
men manipulate other humans may be due to the Russian national
character; in part it may be a consequence of the political dictator-
ship in the Soviet Union. But, an important reason for the difference
between Soviet managers and American managers is the different
level of economic development in the two countries. For, in our
society, human life and next to it personal security, in an economic, but even in an emotional sense, are values of high priority,
whereas in underdeveloped countries, life is cheap and human
happiness of little concern. Such differences in values become
internalized and thus part and parcel of typical behavior patterns
associated with particular roles in a given society.

Although we may be entitled to speak, in a very general sense,
of a managerial personality type as distinct from an entrepreneurial

type the actual manifestations of overt behavior of managers in
societies with widely differing value structures will be different.
This is the reason why it is more difficult to apply conclusions
derived from western managerial behavior to the prospective
forms of managerial activity in underdeveloped countries than
conclusions derived from the examples provided by Russian
managers.

It may be answered that the political aspirations of many presently underdeveloped countries demand the establishment of democratic institutions; that the most important of them, having risen
from the fetters of colonialism, want to banish institutions reminiscent of that period of servitude. Although these observations are
not denied, they do not appear to be decisive. In the past, colonial
governments or investors from the mother countries have found
that management which paid little or no attention to the happiness
of the labor force paid good dividends. In many parts of the world,
virtual slavery was not uncommon, and even where colonial governments showed concern for the welfare of native populations and
attempted to prevent serious exploitation of the natives, the recruitment of laborers and the enforcement of industrial discipline was in
the hands of individuals whose ruthlessness towards, and disregard of,
the human values of their wards have become a popular complaint
of native leaders against the evils of colonialism. Sometimes these
grievances were doubtless exaggerated for propagandistic reasons
but where there is so much smoke, there surely is fire.

Moreover, although the era of colonialism has ended in many
parts of the world, in many tropical countries, life is still cheap and
the living standards of actual or potential laborers so low that it would
be folly to claim a standard of welfare or economic and emotional
security for them in any way approaching those of the workers in

more advanced countries. Harsh and ruthless management has proven efficient in the past and it will be found to be efficient in the future. The Russian revolution was also ushered in with slogans promising the final elimination of human exploitation and of merciless bourgeois employers, and has resulted in a system of servitude the violence of which increased with the stepping up of economic development. Finally, although there are a few noble men who are the spokesmen of the aspirations of the masses in underdeveloped countries for the realization of a humane and secure existence, the upper classes, including many intellectuals in government, are prepared to manipulate the hapless masses in a way similar to that of the foreign masters whose rule is now broken. After all, why should we expect these men to have basically different attitudes than those held by English factory masters and overseers in the early part of the nineteenth century, who did not hesitate to use the strap on the backs of small children if they did not work fast enough or if they fell asleep from exhaustion after fourteen or more hours of work? Both operate in an environment where human labor is abundant, where the masses of people often have to be forcibly adjusted to the discipline and regularity of industrial labor, and where the ruthless and often inhuman manipulation of men brings ample rewards in output, money, or social power.

If, therefore, the managerial tendencies in an underdeveloped country predominate, we are likely to see a repetition of conditions reminiscent of the "Hungry Forties" in England or of contemporary labor relations in the Soviet Union.

Some of these results may, of course, obtain also if entrepreneurial tendencies predominate. The very reference to England at the height of laissez-faire shows that managerial disregard for human values, and managerial ruthlessness for the sake of profit or power are not confined to a system in which business leaders are public officials. But it is here that the advances made in the hundred years since the Hungry Forties, and the experience of colonialism have had an effect. If economic development is carried on to a large extent by private entrepreneurs instead of governments, many of the excesses which were possible in the early nineteenth century will not be possible today. All independent underdeveloped countries have elaborate laws on their statute books, designed to protect laborers and to elevate standards of employment. Although these laws may not always be fully enforced, the ruthless application of tactics of managerial efficiency under wholesale disregard of the welfare of workers often will meet with considerable difficulties.

It would seem, therefore, that from the point of view of human welfare economic development in the form of privately owned small and medium sized plants is preferable to that based chiefly on large public enterprises (9). The crucial question, which I fear cannot be answered fully, but on which some light may perhaps be thrown, is what are the conditions which favor and those which impede the growth and development of private entrepreneurship. In other words, the question may be phrased of whether a "climate" for entrepreneurship can be created in backward countries and what are the conditions which favor it.

II

At first glance it may appear that the conditions for creating a climate of entrepreneurship, at least in some of the largest under-developed countries, is favorable in view of the already existing entrepreneurs in the commercial and money-lending fields. As was pointed out earlier these persons are entrepreneurs already and it may be assumed that they would be the individuals most apt and psychologically most suited to become the carriers of entrepreneurial functions in a developing economy. However, the question may be asked, why, if this is so, they have not in the past participated more fully in productive activity instead of concentrating on trade and banking. A customary answer is that in colonial areas they were prevented from doing so because of their inability to compete with the powerful enterprises domiciled in the mother country. But this answer is hardly convincing. In the first place, such competition was equally severe in commerce and banking. In the second place, if we look at the kind of enterprises which native entrepreneurs did establish in the commercial and money lending field, we find that they were supplementary to similar activities engaged in by large European firms. In other words, the native trader with a middleman between the local native markets, often in outlying districts or distant islands, and the metropolitan export-and-import houses. Also, native traders were engaged in commerce with those localities with which the European houses for various reasons did not care to maintain regular connections. It was similar with money lending. The native operator worked chiefly on the village level, whereas large-scale banking was almost exclusively in the hands of branches established by metropolitan houses.

If these native entrepreneurs were thus supplementing their European "competitors" in these activities, why did they not, in the past, enter more fully into those areas of manufacturing which had a similar relation to firms established and run by Europeans. One would not expect that native entrepreneurs would have entered into competition with foreign-financed mining and transportation companies. But there were and are numerous industrial branches in which ample opportunity exists for the establishment of small-scale plants, which could have played a similar role in relation to the larger foreign-financed enterprises as that of the native trader and money lender to the foreign wholesaler and banker (10).

I believe that there is another reason why the present native money lenders and traders cannot be considered the chief man-power pool out of which industrial entrepreneurs may be recruited. Apparently a strong motivation to make profits is not enough. A person who is to become an industrial entrepreneur must have additional personality traits to those resulting from a drive to amass wealth. A little closer analysis of what is involved in setting up and guiding an industrial establishment will make this clear. The small trader or money lender can operate with few and often without any assistants, whereas an industrial entre-preneur typically must hire a group of men whose labor he must organize and direct. In addition to being motivated by the expec-tation of profit, he must also have some managerial abilities and more important, he must have the ability to lead.

But the most basic distinction between the function of an industrial entrepreneur and one engaged in commercial or financial trans-actions consists in the form of daily activity which the two kinds of entrepreneurial roles require. To put it in a nutshell, the industrial entrepreneur who runs a small plant is a man who gets his hands dirty. In some branches of industry this may occur seldom, in others frequently, but the technical organization of small industry requires that the owner participate fully and often constantly in the actual productive processes. The chief characteristic of a small industrial entrepreneur is not so much his venturesomeness, nor his motivation to make profits, but his capacity to lead other men in a common undertaking and his inclination to introduce innovations; and in the early stages of industrialization, especially when production is carried on by small scale plants, the overwhelming bulk of these innovations are of a technological nature requiring the direct and immediate participation of the entrepreneur.

Moreover, the capital employed by a trader or moneylender turns over much faster than that used in production establishments. A trader may, indeed, carry on his business without ever attaining property rights in the objects he deals with. He may be a broker or commission agent, and run only the risk of losing his earnings from a transaction rather than the capital invested therein. A money lender, or banker, deals in that commodity that has the widest currency, that is accepted by anyone, that can easily be transported, hidden, and that — if need be — can be directly used to bribe officials or other persons in power. An industrial entrepreneur has usually more property tied up in his plant for a longer time than either a trader or a banker; he depends upon the smooth functioning of a market to sell his output; his property is exposed to a series of dangers — destruction by fire or other accidents — which the others may escape. Other things being equal the risks and uncertainties involved in the production of commodities is therefore much greater than in trading and money lending.

It is not easy to produce conclusive evidence for this proposition. The best evidence we have is drawn from the industrial history of developed countries. For example, the provisional results of a study of the social background and certain personality characteristics of early English iron masters, in which I am currently engaged, indicates that these men were chiefly contrivers of new technical procedures, rather than men of commercial and financial genius. Many of them made money, but this was rather due to their attaining a quasi-monopolistic position in the production of certain commodities, than to their unusual business acumen. Similar results appear to hold for early French entrepreneurs, and a survey of German industrial establishments of the early nineteenth century also shows that most of the founders of these plants were men with mechanical rather than financial skills (11).

These men came from the ranks of artisans, laborers, yeomen, and cottagers. A few were sons of middle class and a few sons of upper class parents. And although the moneyed men eventually put their funds into the enterprises, the industrial development was not set off by them. The earliest industrial entrepreneurs were men who worked with their hands, whose innovations were in the field of technology and who, in their majority, came from the lower, propertyless, classes. Only later, when their firms had become successful and had grown to such proportions that the owner need not get his hands dirty, did the financiers and the managers infiltrate into industry. Eventually, they even succeeded in wresting the decisive power positions from the technicians and the chief virtue of a leader of a joint stock company became his financial and organizational aptitude rather than his understanding of the technical production process.

In comparing the types of business leadership which are of importance in an analysis of the economic advancement of underdeveloped countries we have found three forms, each of which is characteristic of a particular role and function in the social fabric of a developing economy, but each of which appears to correspond also to a particular personality orientation. At the two extremes are the managerial and the merchant-money-lender types, between them is the industrial entrepreneur type. All these types of business leadership fit rather well into the classification of character orientations elaborated by Erich Fromm (12). The merchant or money-lender function appears to be most adequately suited to persons with a predominant marketing orientation, the function of managers to persons with predominant authoritarian (exploiting) orientation, and the function of industrial entrepreneurship, although containing elements of the former two, seems to call for an individual with a predominant productive orientation. The creation of a "climate for entrepreneurship" depends, therefore, on the one hand on establishing social institutions which make possible objectively the exercise of independent individual enterprises, and on the other on allowing the maturation and development of personalities whose predominant orientation is in the direction of productivity, working, and creative integration.

The realization of the first condition depends, as already pointed out, on a series of political acts. If rigidities of caste and class structure are mitigated, if government is able to protect property rights efficiently regardless of claims of privilege, and if the administration of laws is assured in an impersonal and reasonably equitable manner, the main objective conditions for the development of creative industrial entrepreneurship are present. But these same political acts are also important preconditions for the development of character orientations favoring industrial entrepreneurship. It is granted that an individual's character orientation is determined in large part by biological needs and the early stages of socialization during infanthood and childhood. But the objective, external conditions, the social structure and political framework of a society within which concrete, overt action is carried on, in turn determines the specific forms which this action takes. There exist many different kinds of concrete sets of action which an individual with a given orientation can and will select.

Some of them may involve a high degree of social approval and hence constitute the "normal" or "preferred" alternatives of social behavior. Others may involve social disapproval, and hence be accompanied by risks of punishment or repudiation. A third group again may be neutral. Since it is impossible for a centralized agency to plan effectively for the kind of personality orientation which is to prevail, the only freedom left for planners who favor a particular set of actions is to create external conditions which will attract individuals with appropriate orientations to engage in certain roles designed to lead to the desired objective. In more concrete terms, if social planning in underdeveloped countries is directed toward stimulating the evolution of free industrial entrepreneurship, it must provide for the establishment of external, objective conditions which will make such entrepreneurial activity an attractive or even strongly approved alternative of social behavior. Similarly, if it is the objective of planners to curtail the evolution of free industrial entrepreneurship, the opposite condition is necessary. This does not necessarily imply that in the second case individuals with a predominantly productive orientation will be nonexistent; but such individuals will be likely to choose other paths of life than industrial entrepreneurship.

This analysis is based on the assumption that entrepreneurship can develop only in a society in which cultural norms permit variability in the choice of paths of life, and in which the relevant processes of socialization of the individual are not so completely standardized and demanding conformity to a prescribed pattern, that the bases for appropriate personality development leading to productive orientation are absent. In more concrete terms, we should expect that the foregoing analysis cannot be applied to small, relatively isolated cultures with a large degree of uniformity in behavior patterns and values. Hence no fruitful conclusions on the possibilities of creating a "climate for entrepreneurship" can be derived from observing and comparing a large number of the most primitive cultures.

But in the larger countries which stand on the threshold of potential economic advancement at a fairly rapid rate, there are large portions of the rural population in which conformity to traditional values is high and in which behavior patterns (and hence processes of socialization of individuals) tend to adhere to stereotype forms. In India, for example, the gap between the adherence to traditional cultural standards in many villages, and the emancipation of urban dwellers from tradition is relatively greater than appears to have been the case in eighteenth century England. In consequence one cannot apply the historical experience, derived from European development in presently underdeveloped countries. Especially, the social background of an emerging entrepreneurial class is not identical, or even similar, to that of the early English, French, or German factory masters.

This variation in social structure and the consequent variation in the manpower pool from which nascent business leaders are recruited may also exercise a strong influence on the type of business leadership and may be one of the crucial factors explaining why individual entrepreneurship had remained seriously limited in the native populations of underdeveloped countries and why the more likely forms of business leadership in these countries may be along managerial rather than entrepreneurial lines.

NOTES TO CHAPTER VI

1. See R. F. Harrod, Toward a Dynamic Economics (London, 1948), p. 16.

2. The most notable works are: Joseph Schumpeter, The Theory of Economic Development (Cambridge, 1934); Colin Clark, The Conditions of Economic Progress, 1st ed. (London, 1940); 2nd ed. (London, 1951); Allan G. B. Fisher, Economic Progress and Social Security (London, 1945); and R. F. Harrod, op. cit.

3. The most extensive study that has come to my notice on the role of human resources in the process of economic growth is the book by Wilbert E. Moore, Industrialization and Labor (New York, 1951). See also J. J. Spengler, "Some Economic Aspects of the Subsidization by the State of the Formation of 'Human Capital'," Kyklos, 4 (1950), pp. 316-43, which although confined to conditions in advanced countries, suggests the value of an analogous study for underdeveloped areas.

4. See Fritz Redlich, "The Business Leader in Theory and Reality," American Journal of Economics and Sociology, 8 (1948-49), pp. 223-24.

5. On capital-saving technological advances which may be extremely relevant to industrial development of underdeveloped countries see the excellent remarks by Yale Frozen, "Adapting to Technological Change," Journal of Business of the University of Chicago, Vol. 24, No. 2 (April 1951), pp. 125-26.

6. Werner Sombart, Die Zukunft des Kapitalismus (Berlin, 1932), pp. 8-9, (translation by the writer).

7. Gregory Bienstock, Solomon M. Schwarz, and Aaron Yugow, Management in Russian Industry and Agriculture (New York, 1944).

8. Ibid., pp. 113-24.

9. It should be remarked parenthetically that public utilities and perhaps a few key industries are likely to be established and owned by the State in all underdeveloped countries. The choice discussed in the text is whether a form of public or private ownership, and with it, managerial or entrepreneurial tendencies are to predominate in the economy as a whole.

10. It is admitted, of course, that artisans exist in underdeveloped countries and that some of them abound in "cottage industries." But the crucial difference between the role of the artisan or the cottager on the one hand and the industrial entrepreneur, on the other, is that the scope of the former's activities are limited by the labor which can be supplied within the family, whereas the latter depends upon the labor of persons with whom he enters into a wage contract. Even the fact that an artisan may sometimes hire one or more journeyman helpers does not alter the difference between the two forms of economic activity

158

fundamentally, because the nature of the group formed by an artisan and his helpers on the one hand, and an entrepreneur and his working force on the other, differs in several fundamental respects.

11. On the founders of German industrial enterprises see the very suggestive study by Henry Witt, Die Triebkräfte des industriellen Unternehmertums vor 100 Jahren und beute (Dissertation, Hamburg, 1929), esp. pp. 6-122.

12. See Erich Fromm, Man for Himself (New York, 1947), pp. 111 ff.

7

THE ROLE OF CITIES IN THE ECONOMIC GROWTH OF UNDERDEVELOPED COUNTRIES (1)

At its twenty-seventh meeting the Institute of Differing Civilizations discussed the problem of urbanization and economic growth, and in the general report summarizing the economic aspects of the problem, R. W. Steel listed nine general propositions which, he believed, met with general approval by the participants of the conference. The second proposition listed by Steel and the explanatory comment appended by him run as follows:

> The growth of population in urban and industrial centres appears to be inevitable if there is economic development, whether by industrialization, by the development of mining, or by the commercialization and improvement of agriculture. If governments desire economic development, they must be prepared to face the consequences and to attempt to mitigate the effects of the concentration of people in restricted built-up areas. Not every town, of course, is an indication of commercial development. There are everywhere historic centers, established centuries ago for religious, social, administrative or other reasons; even these have often grown considerably as a result of the economic progress of the present century (2).

This proposition is quite widely accepted, and many persons, notably when they think of industrialization as a means of economic development, tacitly assume that this is bound up with increasing urbanization. But, although there is much talk of industrialization and urbanization as two processes which are apparently closely and necessarily related, the whole array of forces making for urbanization in developing economies is often left unexamined, various types of urban centers are left undistinguished, and the moral and social-psychological, as well as economic and political, consequences of urbanization are left unexplored. This short paper will attempt to suggest the various problem areas that arise in probing somewhat more deeply into the process of urbanization and the study of towns and cities in underdeveloped countries.

The study of urbanization in relation to economic development has several points of interest. In the first place, it offers a field for the testing of hypotheses on the theory of location. The precise location of new cities may, therefore, be planned, and the findings of the theory of location may be applied to the development of a net of urban settlements in new countries (or new parts of old countries).

Second, and this is also still primarily a problem area in economics, a city may be studied from the point of view of the mobilization of manpower for industrial and other economic development. It is well known that one of the crucial problems in the study of economic development is the determination of conditions under which human resources will be forthcoming for the new productive tasks which the developing economy sets itself. Now it may be said with a good deal of confidence that in underdeveloped countries, notably in those with population pressure on existing agricultural resources, there has been little difficulty, in the past, in obtaining unskilled laborers in sufficient number for new enterprises. The bottlenecks and shortages that existed were due to the limitations of native individuals with adequate training for some complex tasks or to the lack of industrial

discipline in a population still little used to factory work. Though
from the standpoint of efficient resource allocation labor may be
more redundant, and hence cheaper, in the open country than in
cities and towns, urban areas are, nevertheless, the most suitable
places for the establishment of factories, since they are the centers
in which a potential industrial labor force is concentrated. From
the standpoint of the laborer the city provides the possibility of
shifting to other industrial jobs, often — especially in large industrial towns — in the same industry. From the standpoint of
the entrepreneur it makes it unnecessary to select his force from
a group of peasants whom he may have to drill and accustom to
industrial discipline and for whom he often may have to provide
housing and other services. Instead, he can select from a generally floating population that is looking for work in industrial and
other nonagricultural enterprises and, in some cases, even from
a skilled work force that he can attract by offering higher wages
or better working conditions than those prevailing in the industries
in which his prospective workers are now employed. In other words,
in the town or city — and only in the town or city — a labor force
can be found that is finally committed to industry and does not tend
to float back regularly to the land, and this fact makes the labor
contract more impersonal, functionally specific, and tends to en-
dow it with universalistic criteria in the selection of individuals for
for industrial jobs. Labor comes to be regarded more and more as
a commodity, and in the allocation of tasks, status considerations,
kinship ties, and similar noneconomic variables tend to be more
and more disregarded. This in turn leads to a more rational (in
Max Weber's sense of "Zweckrationalitaet") allocation of human
resources.

But the town, and especially the large city, has still another advantage for the location and expansion of nonagricultural enterprises in the greater variety of skills and occupational specialties which can be found there. This factor has the tendency of minimizing bottlenecks due to shortages of certain skilled persons and of facilitating horizontal and vertical expansion of existing nonagricultural enterprises.

All these factors appear to be commonplace, but together they explain why in underdeveloped countries industries tend to concentrate in a limited number of cities, why these cities often grow to very great size, and why many countries entering the path of industrialization have vast agricultural regions with very few industrial islands in them. These factors have the result of sharpening the contrast between city and country, and it is perhaps not inappropriate to regard the cities in underdeveloped regions even as exhibiting a different culture from that of the countryside.

This fact, in turn, leads to a very important question. To what extent is the growth of an urban culture in underdeveloped countries a vehicle for changing the values and beliefs of the society so as to make it more inclined to accept economic growth? It is generally acknowledged that one of the chief barriers to rapid economic advancement in many parts of the world — in spite of the widely prevalent aspirations for economic betterment — is the traditionalism in the social values on the part of the bulk of the population. Using Robert Redfield's terminology, a characteristic of many underdeveloped countries is the relatively high degree of prevalence of a folk-like society which is usually opposed to rapid change and unable to adapt itself quickly enough to the pressures exerted on it by the increasing integration of underdeveloped countries into the world economy. But the cities, even in underdeveloped countries, are modeled, at least in some significant aspects, after the urban centers of the West. They exhibit a spirit different from that of the countryside. They are the main force and the chief locus for the introduction of new ideas and new ways of doing things. One may look, therefore, to the cities as the crucial places in underdeveloped countries in which the adaptation to new ways, new technologies, new consumption and production patterns, and new social institutions is achieved. The main problem remaining is the nature of this adaptation in the various underdeveloped countries and the degree to which the changed culture of the urban centers affects the surrounding "sea" of traditional folk-like ways of life.

So far we have treated urbanization as though it were a process set in motion only by industrialization. But, as already stated in the passage quoted from Steel's paper, this is by no means the case. Although there is a high correlation between industrialization and urbanization, the development of towns and cities is not dependent upon the previous establishment of industries, nor must all industrial establishments be located in cities in order to flourish. Historically, cities have been the seats of learning and education, they have been the centers of governmental and administrative organizations, and they have performed the function of religious or cultural rallying points. In these ways their importance for the survival of a given culture has proved to be much greater than could be assigned to them merely on the basis of population.

Even though often only a small percentage of a country's population inhabited its cities, among this small group could be found the principal carriers of its cultural and intellectual values and the chief holders of its political and economic power. This is probably the most outstanding aspect of cities, and the one most often commented upon. It finds expression as early as the late medieval works which stand at the very beginning of urban sociology. Ibn Khaldûn, writing in the fourteenth century, stressed particularly the view that the city as the seat of a central or provincial government also exhibits economic patterns significantly different from those of the surrounding countryside. Since the proceeds of taxation are accumulated in the cities, and, since governmental and educational functions are concentrated there, new patterns of demand arise. These tend to affect, in turn, the patterns of production and supply, bringing about profound economic differences between country and city. Similar views were expressed some two hundred years later by another "forerunner" of urban sociology, Giovanni Botero. The main difference between the theories of these two writers is the relative emphasis placed on political and on economic factors. Ibn Khaldûn, who lived in Spain and North Africa, places primary emphasis on the fact that cities are centers of government and political power; Botero, who lived in Italy, places more stress on the commercial and industrial features of cities (3).

Modern writers on urban sociology have reiterated these aspects of cities in a more sophisticated and scientific manner, but they have added relatively little to the identification of the essential distinctive features of urban aggregations. This literature, however, points to urban developments in the West as a model by means of which the interaction between urbanization and economic growth can best be studied (4).

One way of exploring differences in urban function and the effects of different types of towns and cities upon the economic and cultural development of the surrounding regions may be through a historical study of the development of the cities of western Europe and their interaction with the economic development of the part of the world in which they were situated.

It is well known that, beginning with the early eleventh century,

Western Europe underwent a process of economic development which was accompanied by growth of towns and urban institutions. This development reached its peak in the late thirteenth and early fourteenth centuries. Many of the old Roman <u>municipia</u> in Italy and Gaul had lost vigor and importance first during the barbarian invasions and later due to the control of Mediterranean trade by the Arabs but had never completely ceased to exist. In the course of this process of development they were revived and began a renewed period of growth. At the same time entirely new towns were founded, and some of them, notably in Flanders and along the North Sea, became of great importance and power and grew to considerable size.

In considering the role played by medieval cities, we may follow the general lines of argument developed by Alfons Dopsch and Henri Pirenne. Few men have been concerned so consistently with this problem, and, although fully aware of the legal and constitutional problems inherent in the history of urban development in medieval Europe, they attached major importance to the economic aspects of urbanization (5).

Like its forerunner in antiquity, the medieval town was a fortified place in which the surrounding rural population could find shelter during periods of war or invasion. But those medieval towns that survived the great Norman raids of the ninth century, or that were founded afterward, had still another function. They were places which had either a special economic or a special political function. The city with a primarily political function Pirenne calls the "Liége" type and the city with a primarily economic function the "Flemish" type. Liége was the seat of an archbishop who ruled over an extended territory. His court, at which were employed a considerable number of officials and administrators and which was

166

supplemented by institutions designed to train priests, administrators of church property, and other "intellectuals," formed the
nucleus of the city. Pirenne describes Liége in the following
words:

> Until the middle of the 14th century Liége was essentially
> a city of priests, bristling with church towers and cut up
> by great monastic precincts. As its clerical population
> increased and the court of the bishop developed, the num-
> ber of artisans necessary for the maintenance of this com-
> munity grew proportionately (6).

In other words, Liége was a town of administrators, bureaucrats, teachers, and students, to whom were added an appropriate
number of artisans and servants supplying them with finished
goods and services. Economically, it was of little importance up
to the fifteenth century, but as a center of political power and a
capital of education it was unequaled for many leagues around. Such
cities as Liége existed in many parts of medieval Europe. Reims
and Laon in France, Utrecht in the northern part of the Low
Countries, and Worms, Mainz, and Speyer in Germany are other
examples. In Britain, the political and educational functions were
separated, and Oxford and Cambridge developed independently of
Westminster. But many important centers maintained a primary
political or educational function not only throughout the Middle
Ages but beyond. Examples of this can be found among the cities
which formed the capitals of later German states, such as Karls-
ruhe or Weimar, or which attained new political importance because
of the consolidation of states, such as Bern, which became the capital of the Swiss confederation.

In contrast to the Liége type of city, there developed in medieval
Europe a city which had primarily an economic function. In fact,
when we think of the typical medieval city, we have in mind the
great emporiums which developed along the Mediterranean and the

North Sea; we think of Bruges or Ghent rather than Liége, of
Marseilles or Rouen rather than Laon, of Lübeck, Venice, or
Genoa rather than Worms or Speyer. In other words, we think
of the medieval city as an institution responding to the economic
rather than the political, educational, or religious needs of
European society.

Yet we must not exaggerate the number of large commercial
and financial centers that existed. In the territory which in the
late nineteenth century formed Germany, there were altogether
some twenty-three hundred "cities." (7) It is not necessary to
point out that many of these places, although endowed with special
rights (Stadtrecht), were not cities in the same sense as Cologne,
Frankfurt, or Augsburg. They were small places, with not more
than two to five thousand inhabitants, which had significance for
the immediate neighborhood in which they were established but
whose radius of effective influence was strictly limited. The
overwhelming majority of medieval cities, not only in Germany but
all over Europe, were of this kind.

Among the larger towns we may distinguish two kinds: the city
with primarily commercial and financial functions and the industrial
city. By far the majority of medieval cities seem to have had
commercial and financial functions. These were the towns whose
power and wealth was based upon their being the home base of a
group of important merchants engaging in international trade or
which were places in which great banking houses were domiciled.
In many instances, merchants and financial families were so closely
related that it is often impossible to distinguish between those towns
which were primarily centers of trade and those which were primarily
banking centers. Examples of cities that performed mercantile and
financial functions are Genoa, Venice, Milan, Marseilles, and

168

Barcelona in the Mediterranean and Hamburg, Breman, Lübeck, Cologne, and later Augsburg and Antwerp in the region north of the Alps.

These cities all present a series of special features, some of which might be worth enumerating. Their government was composed of a small and progressively less open group of wealthy patrician merchant and financial families. Since they had little industry, they had no proletariat comparable to that of the industrial towns. Their social structure was made up of three main classes: the wealthy families, who, as a rule, formed the political elite; artisans and their journeymen, who were usually organized in guilds and thus assured of a standard of life appropriate to their status; and a mass of floating rabble — poor persons, servants, and recent immigrants from the country who found occasional or regular employment but who did not yet form a relatively homogeneous working class such as existed in Europe later in the eighteenth and nineteenth centuries (8).

The few industrial centers exhibit some different features. They are the towns to which Pirenne refers when he speaks of a Flemish type, for the cities of Flanders and a few towns in northern Italy and upper Germany were the only ones before the fifteenth century which were centers of sizeable industries. In the large towns of Flanders and in Florence, we find a textile industry; in upper Germany, we find some textile production; and in Milan and Brescia, we find metallurgical industries. In Venice, in addition to the production of woolen cloth, there was the manufacture of ships and shipping equipment in the large Arsenal of the Republic.

The demand for labor was considerably greater, other things being equal, in an industrial town than in a financial-mercantile center. This demand was met in part by providing more regular employment opportunities for immigrants to the city and, in part, by drawing within the economic compass of the city the inhabitants of villages near it. Here is an instance of the direct impact of the city on changing or "co-ordinating" the economic activity of the region in which it is located. Whether or not the workers within and around these industrial cities may be regarded as a distinct social class is still disputed, but there is no doubt that all groups engaged in industry acquired a political education the hard way, as well as new ambitions. The history of these industrial cities differed from that of mercantile centers probably because of the strong and unified front which the industrially employed population could present. The oligarchy in these cities was broken, or at any rate made insecure, and the result was recurring revolt or the approach to democratic government and a broadening of political power. The war of the textile workers of Bruges against the patrician Lellaerts and the king of France associated with them in the period 1301-28, the struggle of the weavers of Ghent in the 1370's and 1380's against the French crown, and the violent strike of the Florentine ciompi in 1378 (crowning a movement of social unrest which had lasted for over a century) led to a democratization of urban government and a greater participation of the popular classes in the legislatures and hence the destinies of their towns (9).

The main new sets of ideas and practices which were developed by medieval cities may be grouped as follows. On the one hand, there were towns with predominantly political and intellectual functions. New forms of administration, new bureaucracies, new methods of legislation and of international negotiations, and new forms of political behavior on the part of the rulers and their servants were developed. At the same time the town was a center of learning. Knowledge, science, and philosophy were pushed forward in the universities located in larger cities. The town population was more literate than the country population. The town was the place in which a nascent intelligentsia was formed, at first composed exclusively of clerics, but later, even before the Reformation, it gradually became more and more secular, culminating in the group of rationalist humanists of the sixteenth century (10).

Apart from their political and intellectual function, cities had a predominant economic function. They were the places in which new forms of economic activity and new types of economic organization were evolved. They were the places not merely in which new commodities were traded and whence new markets and sources of supply were explored and conquered but in which appeared the first signs of new class relations based on alterations in the social division of labor. And, for all the differences in national temperament, religious beliefs, customs, and historic circumstances, Bruges and Ypres are the true forerunners of Manchester and Bradford; they are the textile towns of medieval Europe.

This sketch of the kinds of medieval towns and the functions of urban centers contains an enumeration of culture complexes for whose change the existence of sizeable towns or cities appears to be an indispensable requirement. The impact of cities in these fields has been felt in the Western world in an enhanced fashion in the period since the end of the Middle Ages. Especially with the growth of manufacturing industries in the seventeenth and eighteenth centuries, the industrial city has been given a powerful impetus, and we have come to associate industrialization and urbanization as part and parcel of one and the same process. But even while the new industrial cities of Lancashire and the Ruhr mushroomed, the con-

solidation of national states in Europe aided the growth of political capitals, commercial centers, and port towns. The medeival
dichotomy between Liége and Bruges has its modern counterpart
in the dichotomies between The Hague and Amsterdam, Rome and
Milan, Bern and Zurich. At the same time such giants as London,
Paris, and Berlin, and other cities of similar size elsewhere,
exhibit a multitude of aspects. The capitals of many European
countries are urban areas in which commercial, financial, industrial, intellectual, and political functions are combined, so
that it would be difficult to "type" a place like London or Paris.
But this is the outcome of the high degree of co-ordination made
possible by modern administrative techniques and a business
technology facilitating the most minute division of labor. It is
also due to the large concentration of many millions of persons in
a relatively small space made possible by the development of
transportation facilities and new technology in housing and city
planning. The multifunction city, such as London or Paris, is
clearly a modern phenomenon, although some vestiges of this
type of city can be found as far back as the sixteenth century.

This suggests several different problems which might be elu-
cidated by a closer study of urbanization and economic growth in
their historical dimensions. On the one hand, we may discern a
growing diversification of urban functions with advancing technology
which makes feasible communication within a city and between it
and an increasingly larger surrounding region. Just as modern
technology permits the development of vast and complex businesses,
so it permits the development of vast and complex multifunction
cities. At the same time, and I believe as a consequence of the
more conscious application of principles of the theory of location,
we witness an increasing specialization of cities in the kinds of

products they supply and often in the type of economic function they
fulfill. An example is the establishment of specialized cities in the
U. S. S. R. during the last twenty years. Thus we may witness two
opposing trends, one affecting chiefly the very large metropolitan
centers which tend to give up specific urban functions and to adopt
many different functions; the second affecting smaller cities which
tend to develop new forms of specialized functions — for example,
the university town, the resort town, the steel town, the port,
the railroad center.

In view of this, the problems which we discovered in studying
medieval urban development are repeated in part in presently
underdeveloped countries. I have given this sketch of the forms
and functions of medieval cities, not because I believe that precisely
the same forms and functions can be found in the underdeveloped
countries of today, but to show, by means of an example, how the
study of the development and growth of towns in an economically
underdeveloped area (such as medieval Europe) can shed important
light on the over-all conditions and processes of economic development.

There exist, as I hope will be admitted, many parallels between
the European Middle Ages and presently underdeveloped countries.
For example, in many parts of the world we have the functional
division between political-intellectual urban centers and economic
centers. Delhi and Bombay, or Quito and Guayaquil, and to some
extent even Rio de Janeiro and São Paulo, or Peiping and Shanghai,
are instances of this difference. At the same time, however, large
urban settlements are so sparse in many underdeveloped countries
that many of those that have developed are multipurpose cities.
Jakarta, Rangoon, and most capitals of Latin-American countries
are examples.

But these distinctions have been made not to obtain criteria by which towns and cities can be classified but rather to obtain a series of variables important for economic development which require for their full unfolding an urban environment. Commerce, financial institutions, industrial establishments, governmental bureaucracies, and advanced educational and intellectual training facilities all require an urban climate to develop and flourish. Our first problem is to see whether we can discern significant differences in the occupational structure and social composition of different cities in underdeveloped countries and to try to determine whether any regularities can be ascribed to such differences. Benares and Ahmedabad are both cities of several hundred thousand inhabitants in India. Yet I am convinced that a careful sociological survey of the two would show considerable differences between them. If these differences can be ascertained, let us then proceed to make hypotheses concerning the characteristics of different cities which are relevant to different aspects of economic development. In some instances an industrial environment may be wanted, but in others the impetus for the formation of a critically minded intelligentsia or an impersonal, honest, efficient bureaucracy may be just as important preconditions of economic development. In our preoccupation with the close association between industry and urbanization, we often tend to forget that underdeveloped countries need not only industries but also other social, political, and intellectual innovations which may be fostered more effectively in nonindustrial urban centers.

Posing the problem in this way leaves open the question of the relation between industrialization and the development of efficient governmental services. Historically, the two trends appear to have been closely associated, although it would probably be difficult

to say which exercised the determining influence. In Prussia,
modern forms of public administration preceded industrialization.
In Britain and, to a lesser extent, in France they lagged behind.
But, regardless of the precise historical sequence, the net effect
in all cases was an increase in average real income, which also
strongly affected the nonurban regions located near the centers of
development. This process has recently been described by T. W.
Schultz (11). His essay, though addressed explicitly to another
problem, contains a set of theoretical generalizations of the first
importance for the study of the interrelations between urbanization
and economic growth. The problems raised by Schultz form a
bridge to the questions discussed in the succeeding paragraphs.

Our second task is to investigate the over-all impact which
urban centers have under modern conditions of economic development. Two men whose social views are diametrically opposed
both testify to the overwhelming importance of the difference between town and country. Marx pointed to this "antithesis" in
many of his works and, in Capital, even went so far as to state
that "the whole economical history of society is summed up in the
movement of this ... separation between town and country." (12)
M. I. Rostovtzeff, who, as is well known, was and is an ardent
anti-Marxist, introduced a course of lectures he gave in 1922
with the following words:

> What is my purpose in giving this short introduction to your
> work? It is to interpret one of the main problems of modern
> economic and social life.... The problem I mean is the prob-
> lem produced by the existence in our social life of two dif-
> ferent types of men, the country people and the city people.
> Of course, these two types exist in this country also, but, as
> far as I know, there is no such sharp antagonism, so sharp
> a contrast between these two types as there is, for example,
> in Russia and to a lesser extent in Western Europe (13).

Both Marx and Rostovtzeff had in mind, above all, differences

in the typical form of economic organization characteristic of urban and rural economic activity. The city, the factory with its
proletarian labor force, and the sharp distinction between workers,
middle class, petty bourgeoisie, and entrepreneurial groups (enhanced in pre-World War I Russia and strongly marked in nineteenth-
century Europe) were contrasted with the economic and social order
of the countryside. There the typical productive unit was small
and normally required the participation of the members of only one
family, and the landlord was opposed to the small owner-farmer
or tenant farmer. The middle class and, above all, the intelligentsia
were not indigenous to the countryside; and whatever officials, teachers,
or other intellectuals resided there had migrated from urban areas.

The economic organization of the city represented the predominant
form of capitalist economy; that of the countryside still contained
many elements of precapitalistic economic forms. On the purely
economic level, therefore, differences were clearly discernible in
institutions, forms of productive organization, occupational specialization, and social structure as it related to economically differentiated
groups. Within limits, these contrasts could be interpreted as representing an aspect of a dual economy, such as has been found to exist
in some underdeveloped countries. The difference between Marx's
analysis of nineteenth-century western Europe and Rostovtzeff's analysis of early twentieth-century Russia, on the one hand, and the picture
of the urban-rural contrast in medieval Europe outlined in this paper,
on the other hand, does not lie in the fact that the contrast had disappeared. Rather the difference is that in the Middle Ages the cities
were still struggling for recognition, and urbanism as a way of life
was as yet the exception, whereas in the later period capitalism
centered on urban areas was the predominant form of socioeconomic
organization, and the way of life of the city had won out over that of
the country.

But the contrast between city and country is not confined to economic organization alone. Although they do not expressly state it, all the writers who note this contrast imply that it is more far-reaching than is reflected merely in differences in productive organization and forms of economic activity. When Marx says that the antagonism between town and country is one of the main forces in history and when Rostovtzeff says that there are two different types of men, the city people and the country people, they have in mind two cultural types which are opposed to each other. I have mentioned earlier the cultural dichotomy between countryside and city in non-Western societies. This difference is confirmed by observers in many parts of the world. For example, Boeke notes it in Indonesia (where he discusses it as an important aspect of what he calls the "dual society"), Steel mentions it for Africa, and Redfield has described cultural differences between localities exhibiting different degrees of urbanism in Yucatán by applying to them a yardstick derived from the typological contrast between folk and urban culture (14).

Redfield's typology has proved very fruitful for his analysis of the different forms of cultural integration found in urban centers and rural villages, but it suffers from a shortcoming of which he is by no means unaware. Rather than working out the independent determination of two contrasting ideal types, Redfield developed only the type of the folk society and assigned to the urban society all those characteristics which are nonfolk-like. In other words, in Redfield's schema, the urban society is really the nonfolk society.

Redfield would not deny that differences exist between urban centers, but his schema does not penetrate them, because it was not designed to do so. From what has been said earlier, it will be clear that I do not suggest that working out a model of a unique

urban culture is easy or even possible. The difficulty in constructing even an ideal-type model of urban culture is due to that
fact that its outstanding characteristic is its heretogeneity and that,
therefore, sets of culture traits found in the urban centers of one
country need not be repeated in those of another country. Urban
cultures may vary with differences in geographical location or
with differences in the general level of advancement of the countries in which different cities are located. Hence, if it is our
aim to stipulate a single-type of urban culture, as contrasted to
a single ideal-typical folk culture, the only possible procedure is
to choose the path which Redfield used and to describe the urban
culture as exhibiting a series of traits which are the opposite of
related traits found in the folk culture. Thus, the method chosen
imposes by necessity our constructing the urban culture as a nonfolk culture.

For our problem, that is, the determination of the relationship
between urbanism and economic development, it is, however, not
necessary to stipulate a single type of urban culture. In fact, I
believe that this would be a wrong procedure altogether. Whereas
Redfield was interested in determining the forces which made for
cultural stability and integration, economic development provokes
social and cultural change, and our primary attention is directed,
therefore, to forces which may disturb (temporarily or even
permanently) cultural homogeneity and close integration of fairly
uniform folkways. The analysis of the role of cities in the Middle
Ages shows that there appear to be several points of vulnerability
of traditional action patterns and that cities which have different
primary functions are the principal places where the critical changes
occur. But there is one important difference between medieval
cities and cities in contemporary underdeveloped countries. The

former were indigenous adaptations to new forms of economic activity and new types of productive organization. In this way their social structures and over-all functions were, in general, fairly uniform and simple. But the cities of contemporary underdeveloped countries are hybrid institutions, formed in part as a response to the indigenously developing social division of labor and in part as a response to the impact made upon less advanced countries by their integration into the world economy. The urban areas of underdeveloped countries are the chief centers of cultural contact, and the different degree of interpenetration of diverse cultural traits in the cities of different underdeveloped countries, or sometimes even in different cities of the same underdeveloped country, is the chief reason why the characteristics of urbanism (and hence the models for an ideal-typical urban culture) vary from country to country.

In view of the fruitfulness of Redfield's typology for analyzing the characteristics of the folk society, some suggestions he has made for the analysis of different types of urban cultures should be followed up. The modern urban community, as opposed to the folk society, is perhaps more clearly defined as "an aggregate of populations and institutions in civilizational arrangement," whereas the recently formed, rapidly growing city emerging now in many underdeveloped countries may be regarded as "a recent assemblage of folklike societies" (15). This already establishes two, perhaps focal, types of urban culture. It is an empirical question to determine the extent to which features characteristic of one type are present in the other. Even in our most modern cities, folklike traits may be found in the relationships existing in certain ethnic or linguistic neighborhoods, religious communities, or other institutions. At the same time, some of the characteristic features of Western urban centers culturally furthest removed from the folk society, such as interpersonal relations based purely on an economic nexus or anonymity between members of productive or political associations, can be found in many cities of underdeveloped countries. These complexes, as well as differences in the relations of different cities with their hinterland, are variables which must be considered in working out a more definitive typology of urban cultures relevant for the study of the impact of cities on economic growth.

Since our uncertainties and doubts about these problems are due mainly to the scarcity of data, the first and chief task in the study of the role of urbanization in economic growth is the need to initiate a number of surveys of urban institutions and the social and occupational composition of different urban centers in underdeveloped countries. Only a few such surveys exist, and many of these are inadequate (16). On the basis of data on the occupational and social structure of cities in a variety of underdeveloped countries, with different social functions (ports, railroad centers, industrial centers, administrative and governmental centers, and multifunction cities), further hypotheses on the relation between economic growth and urbanization could be formulated. Such surveys should include also an analysis, wherever possible, of the changing aspects of observed economic variables with changes in the size of the city and changes in its over-all social function, if such change has occurred.

The second set of problems which these surveys of the cities of underdeveloped countries should cover is the nature of their growth. Are cities a melting pot for rural populations coming from many parts of their countries? To what extent do immigrants into the city tend to remain there and permanently adopt an urban way of life? What contacts do they maintain with their original home, and what impact do they exert on the places from which they came? Do they tend to migrate to the larger urban areas directly from the villages or by stages through temporary residence in smaller provincial towns? What changes in family structure, religious views, political affiliations, and class or caste status are associated with these migrations? These are a few of the questions which appear important in learning more about the social and cultural changes to which persons gaining contact with urban areas become subjected and in determining the dimensions of the cultural differences between city life and rural life in the various underdeveloped countries.

The third area of study which might produce fruitful results is the comparative study of urbanization processes in currently underdeveloped countries and similar processes in the history of advanced countries, especially in Western Europe. This is not a plea to relearn the "lessons of history," and I am fully aware that the conditions under which, for example, the mining region in South Wales was peopled and developed economically in the later eighteenth and nineteenth centuries differ in many ways from the related process in the Rand mining region in South Africa. The study of urbanization processes in Europe may, however, draw attention to a series of social and economic facts which are often obscured in the underdeveloped countries because of differences in speed of urbanization and because of the contrast between the culture of the immigrant from a remote village and that which he meets in an already partly "Westernized" city. There are many problems which play a significant part in the process of transforming peasants and primitives into city people. Among them are the need to overcome forces fostering anomie on the part of the immigrant who is torn loose from an environment in which he felt secure and thrown into a city where impersonal forces

predominate and primary groups outside the immediate family are
scarce or absent; the problems of adjustment of these immigrants,
who may be regarded as culturally marginal, to a new form of
life; and the intermingling of ethnic or linguistic groups which often
provokes the establishment of new quasi-caste relations (17). These
are among the important factors making for the vulnerability to
radical social and political programs to which workers in newly
formed industrial centers are often subject. They are among the
main background forces at work determining the forms of social
organization that will prevail in the urban centers of a culture —
centers which tend to impress their characteristics on the rest of
the society as it undergoes economic growth.

On the basis of these studies a series of more detailed theoretical
generalizations could probably be made about the impact exerted by
processes of urbanization on economic growth and the problems of
the emergence of urban culture and its association with economic
change. Whether we shall be able to stipulate some unique set of
culture traits as characteristic of urban culture is uncertain. It
might be possible to do so, if those traits were stated in such general terms as to be of little usefulness to practical research. We
may find that the urban cultures of the underdeveloped countries in
South Asia differ from those in, say, Latin America or the United
States; we may find that the culture of industrial cities, such as
Monterrey or Ahmedabad, differs from that of administrative centers,
such as Delhi or Quito; or we may find that the culture of some of
multifunction capitals in underdeveloped countries differs from that
of some of the smaller towns with one primary function. But, even
if we find these diversities, we shall still be able to judge more ac-
curately what impact is exercised by urbanization and its different
forms on the progress and destiny of the peoples in the less advanced
parts of the world.

NOTES TO CHAPTER VII

1. I gratefully acknowledge the assistance given by my colleagues, E. C. Hughes, M. B. Singer, Sylvia Thrupp, and R. R Wohl, who made extensive comments on an earlier draft. None of them is, of course, responsible for the text as it appears here.

2. R. W. Steel, "Economic Aspect: General Report," in International Institute of Differing Civilizations, Record of the XVIIth Meeting Held in Florence (Brussels 1952), p. 120.

3. See Ibn Khaldûn, The Muguddimah, edited and translated by Franz Rosenthal (New York, 1958), II, pp. 235-304; and Giovanni Botero, Delle cause della grandezza e magnificenza delle citta (first published in 1588), reprinted in an edition prepared by Carlo Morando of Botero's Della ragion di Stato (Bologna, 1930), pp. 315-82. An English translation of this work by Robert Peterson appeared under the title A Treatise, concerning the causes of the Magnificencie and greatnes of Cities (London, 1606). For Botero's views on "urban sociology" see especially pp. 322-25 and 346-72 of the Italian edition cited and pp. 9-14 and 41-86 of the English translation.

4. See, for example, Adna Ferrin Weber, The Growth of Cities, "Columbia University Studies in History, Economics and Public Law," Vol. XI (New York, 1899); and especially Max Weber, Wirtschaft und Gesellschaft (3d ed.; Tübingen, 1947), Part III of Grundriss der Sozialökomomik, II, 514-44.

5. See Alfons Dopsch, The Economic and Social Foundations of European Civilization (London, 1937), pp. 303-57; Henri Pirenne, Medieval Cities (Princeton, 1925), and many other writings. All of Pirenne's works on medieval urban life have been brought together in the collection Les Villes et les institutions urbaines (2 vols.; Paris, 1939).

6. Henri Pirenne, Belgian Democracy, Its Early History (Manchester, 1915), p. 101. Dopsch, although he does not use the concepts "Liége" and "Flemish" type, makes the same distinction (op. cit., pp. 318-26).

7. Karl Bücher, "Die Grosstädte in Gegenwart und Vergangenheit," in Th. Petermann (ed.), Die Grosstadt (Dresden, 1903), p. 21.

8. It should be noted that the discussion in the text relates primarily to the cities on the continent of Europe. Sylvia Thrupp has shown that the degree of social mobility in medieval London was very high and that the merchants, above all, formed a class with exceptional social fluidity. See The Merchant Class of Medieval London (Chicago, 1948), passim, esp. chap. v. As Miss Thrupp indicates, there may be a significant difference between London and the cities of the Continent (ibid., p. 191), and the descriptions which we have of some great commercial-financial cities of Italy and Germany seem to confirm the statement of the limited possibilities of ascent to the uppermost social group made in the text. Cf., for example,

for Cologne, Gustav Schmoller, Deutsches Städtewesen in älterer Zeit
(Bonn, 1922), p. 74; for German medieval cities in general, Georg von
Below, Das ältere deutsche Städtewesen und Bürgertum (Bielefeld, 1898),
pp. 118 ff.; for some cities in France, Ch. Petit-Dutaillis, Les Communes
françaises (Paris, 1947), pp. 150 ff.; for Venice, Charles Diehl, Une
république patricienne: Venise (Paris, 1931), pp. 81-119; and for the cities
of Flanders and Italy in general, J. Lestoquoy, Les Villes de Flandre
et d'Italie sous le gouvernement des patriciens (Paris, 1952).

9. An adequate history of medieval social revolutionary and social reform
movements is yet to be written. On the "heroic" period of Bruges see, e.g.,
J. Parneel, Une page detachée de l'histoire de Flandre: 1301-1328 (Bruges,
1850), and, above all, H. Pirenne, Le Soulèvement de la Flandre Maritime
de 1323-1328 (Brussels, 1900), pp. i-lxx. On the revolutions in Florence see,
for example, Niccoló Rodolico, La Democrazia fiorentina nel suo tramonto
(1378-1382) (Bologna, 1905), esp. Part I, chaps. i and iii; Part II,
chaps. i-iii. The underlying sociological differences between oligarchic-
aristocratic and popular-democratic medieval towns have been described
by Max Weber (op. cit., pp. 544-83), who designates the two types of
towns as "Geschlecterstadt" and "Plebejerstadt." The latter he also
regards as the prototype of the modern industrial city.

10. An interesting connection between the medieval businessman and
the intellectuals of the Renaissance is drawn by Yves Renouard, Les
Hommes d'affaires italiens du Moyen Âge (Paris, 1949), esp. pp. 171 ff.

11. Theodore W. Schultz, "Reflections on Poverty within Agriculture,"
Journal of Political Economy, Vol. 58, No. 1 (February, 1950), pp. 1-15.

12. See Karl Marx, Capital (Chicago, 1903), I, 387.

13. Michael I. Rostovtzeff, "Cities in the Ancient World," in Richard
T. Ely (ed.), "Urban Land Economics" (Ann Arbor, 1922), p. 18 (mimeo-
graphed).

14. See J. H. Boeke, "Oriental Economics" (New York, 1947) (mimeo-
graphed), passim, esp. chap. i; Steel, op. cit.; Robert Redfield, The
Folk Culture of Yucatán (Chicago, 1941), chap. ii, and "The Folk Society,"
American Journal of Sociology, Vol. 52, No. 4 (January, 1947), pp. 293-308.

15. These two definitions are taken from an unpublished seminar outline by Professor Redfield. Needless to say, the concept "civilization"
in the first definition relates to the characteristic aspects of modern
Western culture.

16. Among surveys of cities in underdeveloped countries which have
come to my attention are S. D. Gamble, Peking: A Social Survey (New
York, 1921); Richard M. Morse, "São Paulo in the 19th Century: Economic Roots of the Metropolis," Inter-American Economic Affairs, Vol. V,
No. 3 (winter, 1951); Lucila Herrmann, "Clase Media em Guaratinguetá,"
in Theo R. Crevenna (ed.), Materiales para el estudio de la clase media
en la América Latina (Washington, 1950), III, 18-59; N. V. Sovani, Social
Survey of Kolhapur (Nos. 18, 23, and 24 of the "Publications of the Gokhale
Institute of Politics and Economics"), (Poona, 1951-52); and Roger Le

Tourneau, Fès avant le protectorat (Casablanca, 1949); Horace Miner, The Primitive City of Timbuctoo (Princeton, 1953).

17. On this problem see the very stimulating remarks by Everett C. Hughes, "Queries concerning Industry and Society Growing Out of Study of Ethnic Relations in Industry," American Sociological Review, Vol. 14, No. 2 (April, 1949), pp. 211-20.

8

GENERATIVE AND PARASITIC CITIES *

This paper has a threefold purpose. It is supposed to
be a critical summing up of the preceding discussion; it should
attempt to state a general theory of the relations between urbanization and economic growth and cultural change; and it should
suggest some lines along which further fruitful research might be
undertaken in order to obtain more precise knowledge about the
interrelations of the processes of urban growth and development
and those of economic progress and cultural change. This is a
very ambitious task and one which, I fear, I am not able to fulfill
satisfactorily. But I hope that my comments on these three topics
might prove fruitful for further discussion.

There is agreement among the authors of the preceding papers
that the growth and development of cities is a necessary condition
of economic development. Lampard, in particular, points to the
need for greater specialization of tasks which has been associated
invariably with urban centers; Kolb stresses the need for a uni-
versalist-achievement-oriented value structure which is indispensable for a successful rationalization of production, and hence for
industrialization, and finds also that the urban environment was a
necessary condition for the evolution of such values; Davis and

185

Hertz re-echo these views and show that the concentration of economic activities within the relatively narrow geographical space of a
city creates important savings which make possible a greater degree
of specialization of production because of the closeness of comple-
mentary producers. This, in turn, is supported by Lampard's
analysis of external economies to the firm and to the industry,
which creates a situation of decreasing costs and stimulates further specialization. Supplementary to this process of progressive
specialization is the development of new service industries, the
growth of which is correlated with the size of cities, on the one
hand, and the level of income on the other. The former is discussed by Vining and treated more exhaustively by the protagonists
of the theory of urban hierarchy. In the table, which Vining cites
from Brush's study of southwestern Wisconsin, the proliferation
of specialized tertiary industries with increasing size of the central places is clearly shown. Yet this table includes only central
places of the lowest three orders and it need hardly be pointed out
that higher-order central places would exhibit not merely a larger
population, but also a much greater variety of specialized service
industries. The correlation between level of income and relative
preponderance of service industries has been emphasized especially by Colin Clark (1), but it is implicit in the discussion of
Davis and Hertz, Lampard, and Vining. In terms of a theory embracing the concepts of urban hierarchy it can be stated by saying
that higher-order central places are spaced more closely together
in countries with higher incomes than in countries with lower incomes, and that the population of higher-order central places forms
a larger proportion of the total population in countries with higher
incomes than in countries with lower incomes. This result is confirmed by the comparative data on the proportion of urban popu-

lation to total population calculated by Davis and Hertz. Stated in very simple and commonplace terms, this may be expressed by saying that the richer a country, the more urbanized it is and the larger a city in any country the wealthier it is.

It would seem, therefore, cities have, on the whole, exercised a generative function on real income and that, in the light of the available evidence, it is wrong to speak of a "parasitism" or urban centers. But in spite of the apparently overwhelming evidence offered by the study of urban history and the world-wide comparative analysis of urban centers, it may be useful to open up the problem once more.

If we speak of "generative" and "parasitic" cities, we must first explain these concepts. A city may be considered generative of many things, some of them desirable and others undesirable. As has been shown by the authors of the preceding papers, cities have been important centers providing an impetus for economic growth and cultural change, but also a fertile soil has been found in cities for social disorganization, criminality, and other presumably undesirable forms of social behavior. Cities have generated economic progress and crime; they have been places where new forms of cultural adaptation were hammered out, but also where an old culture which had lost vigor and vitality found its last stronghold and refuge. In order to avoid confusion and uncertainty, it is therefore important to state explicitly from what viewpoint a city will be regarded as "generative" or as "parasitic." The answer to this question should be clear from the context in which this paper is written. A city will be designated as generative if its impact on economic growth is favorable, i.e., if its formation and continued existence and growth is one of the factors accountable for the economic development of the region or country in which it

is located. A city will be considered as parasitic if it exerts an
opposite impact. A parallel relation may be stipulated between
the formation and continued existence of a city and cultural change.
If we apply this definition to the classification of cities which
Redfield and Singer present, we must conclude that cities of heterogenetic transformation tend to generate cultural change, whereas
cities of orthogenetic transformation tend to limit, and in the
extreme, may fully impede cultural change. But this does not mean
that orthogenetic cities are necessarily parasitic with regard to
economic growth. The process of primary urbanization, though
leading to a reinforcement of existing cultural patterns, may be
generative of economic growth, and, at the same time, it is
thinkable that cities in certain stages of secondary urbanization
may exert an unfavorable effect upon economic growth of the wider
geographical unit of which they form a part.

In the view of Redfield and Singer the process of primary urbanization is characterized by the development of a Great Tradition.
This is in its core an intellectual process which is viewed as leading
to the development of a class of literati, the final redaction of
"sacred texts" and the evolution of a hierarchy of social control
which often also is interpreted as being based on some sacred
order. But the development of a Great Tradition may often --
though not necessarily always -- be bound up with the release of
forces which exert a beneficial effect on economic growth. This
appears to be suggested by the very definition of the process of
primary urbanization, as implying a certain alteration in the essentially rural small-scale folk society. Historically this process has
been associated with the evolution of often large and powerful empires.
I am not competent to discuss the cultural, intellectual, and general
social trends involved in the development of a great tradition among

the Chinese, Indians, Maya, or several other peoples referred to
by Redfield and Singer. But it is generally acknowledged that the
formation of the great tradition in the ancient river valley civilizations of Egypt and Mesopotamia led not merely to the development of complex religious systems and governmental organizations,
but also to scientific and technological innovations which played an
important role in the more rational exploitation of agricultural resources and the increase in the total product. Similarly the process
of primary urbanization which occurred in the early Middle Ages
in towns which formed the seat of an ecclesiastical lord exerted
often a favorable initial impact on the conditions of economic growth.
In fact the ultimate rise in the late Middle Ages of many free cities,
which originated as seats of a bishop or archbishop, was inaugurated
by the "defection" of the bishop's ministeriales in the struggle between the merchants and artisans and their ecclesiastical over-
lords (2).

Let us now take a look at the obverse situation, one in which a
city is in the stage of secondary urbanization, i.e., undergoes culturally heterogenetic transformation, but at the same time exerts
an unfavorable impact upon economic development of the wider geographical unit of which it forms a part. Redfield and Singer mention,
among others, as typical examples of cities in the heterogenetic
order, certain colonial administrative centers. Several of these
cities may be regarded as forming exclaves of the countries in
which they are located and as contributing to a stagnation -- albeit
often only a temporary stagnation -- of the economic growth of their
countries. Examples for this situation can be found more often in
the past history of colonialism than in the present. The early urban settlements of the various European nations in the New World,
but also in parts of South and South East Asia, appear to have been

of that kind. It is granted that the new techniques introduced by the colonizing power, the increase of trade and commerce carried on by the Europeans, did result in economic growth within the city itself and its immediate environs. But the advantages accruing from this kind of urban growth to the wider region in which such a city was located were counterbalanced by an excessive depletion of natural resources, and the exploitation of peasants and other primary producers. This had the consequence that often stagnation and economic decline rather than economic growth of the region as a whole ensued.

We thus obtain four possible classes into which cities may be placed. They may foster both economic growth and cultural change, they may foster cultural change but exert an unfavorable impact upon the economic development of their hinterland, they may foster economic growth but resist cultural change, and they may induce economic stagnation and impede cultural change at the same time. It may be, of course, that one or more of these "boxes" will prove to be empty. It should also be stressed that any one city may be placed into more than one class in the course of its history. For example, it would appear on first sight that ancient Rome during its stages of primary urbanization tended to affect economic growth favorably, that it continued to do so during the early years of the Empire, although it had entered the stage of secondary urbanization, and that in the last two centuries of the Western Roman Empire it was a factor contributory to the economic decline and stagnation of Italy and other parts of the Roman West. Whether or not this impression can be verified would depend upon a careful and exhaustive analysis of the impact exercised by Rome upon the general level of economic activity of the empire of which it was the capital.

If we accept the distinction between an orthogenetic and a hetero-

genetic urbanization process, and if we admit that a city may at
certain times of its history impede rather than react favorably
upon economic growth, we are faced with two problems. I. The
period during which a city exerts a generative (or conversely a
parasitic) impact may be of unequal duration. We may speak of
a generative (or parasitic) impact in the short run or in the long
run. The meaning of the concepts of short run and long run in
this context is not quite identical with the usage of these terms
by Redfield and Singer nor with the meaning attached to them in
standard economic analysis. Short run relates to a period which
may have some duration, but the end of which may be foreseen
with a high degree of probability. Long run, on the other hand,
designates a period which may be expected to continue indefinitely.
This distinction may be expressed more precisely perhaps in the
following terms. We will speak of a short-run generative (or
parasitic) impact of a city if we can observe the presence of
formation of factors which may be expected with a high degree
of probability to change that impact. We will speak of a long-
term impact, if such factors are not present or in formation.

Before I proceed it may perhaps be useful to make these distinctions clearer by one or two examples. I have mentioned
earlier the impact of the establishment of colonial capitals. They
initiated usually a culturally heterogenetic cycle of urbanization
but at the same time exerted an unfavorable influence on the potentialities of economic growth of the surrounding country. The
founding of Batavia is an instance of such a culturally generative
but economically parasitic process of urbanization (3). Many of
the settlements of the British East India Company in India should
be placed into the same class, and also Spanish colonial capitals
in Mexico and elsewhere in Latin America. The processes un-

leashed in all these urban centers were similar. The old native
ruling class was deprived of power; the desire on the part of the
Europeans to attain a monopoly in the trade of the colony led to
the destruction or debasement of the native merchant class; the
country was exploited by the colonizing power with the sole view
of yielding a maximum of profit to it.

But the divergent trends of economic development within these
cities and outside them, in the wider countryside, had the effect
of creating a situation which tended to counteract and eventually
turn the parasitic impact of these cities into its opposite. The increasing difference in the average income which could be earned
in the city as compared with the countryside tended to attract
migrants, or at least discouraged many who had come to visit
the city to return to their homes. The population of the city
swelled, a labor force came into existence which served not merely
the trading and domestic service needs of the foreigners, but
which made the establishment of industry attractive. This in turn
exerted a favorable influence upon the potentialities of economic development of the wider countryside in which the raw materials for
the industries, which had developed in the cities, were produced.
It also created increased demand for food, and in some instances,
export crops. The net result was the gradual improvement of economic conditions in the countryside and the widening of economic development over an increasing area affecting a growing proportion
of the population outside the city.

This process is described here in its most idealized and simple
form. In some cases it has not yet gone very far and the masses
of the people in many colonial and ex-colonial countries are still
miserably poor. Moreover, in some of the most important underdeveloped countries in which colonial capitals and a few subsidiary

administrative centers formed such parasitic exclaves the attainment of independence brought about a new process of urban growth
which occurred in response partly to political insecurity and warfare in some parts of the country. This wave of urbanization which
can be witnessed in most nonindustrialized countries is a very recent development. It has been noted by Davis and Hertz, who present data for Africa south of the Sahara. Similar processes of
rapid urban growth can be observed in most countries of South
Asia, Latin America, and the Middle East. I shall return later
to this phenomenon.

The parasitic impact of colonial capitals and other administrative centers may be regarded as having been a short run impact in the sense in which this term is employed here. Although
for a time the city tended to exert a clearly unfavorable influence
on the potentialities of economic development of its hinterland,
we saw that factors of change developed in and around the city
which had the effect of turning the parasitic character of the city
into a generative one.

It is not easy to discover actual instances in which the city has
exerted a long-run parasitic influence on the economic development
of the region which it dominated. I have referred earlier to the
decline of ancient Rome in the fourth and fifth centuries, but I also
pointed out that the determination of whether this is a conclusive
case of long-run parasitism in the field of economic development
could be verified only if the history of the impact of the city of Rome
on Italy and the Western Empire were studied more extensively with
this problem in mind. At the time of the decline of the Western
Roman Empire, Rome was, of course, a city with clearly heterogenetic cultural orientation. Though one might be inclined to think
that the historical development of Rome presents a somewhat unique

situation and that one would encounter examples of long-run parasitism with regard to economic growth in cities which have become
the strongholds of a Great Tradition and therefore resist the in-
trusion of culture elements from the outside, most actual examples
of long-run parasitism that come to mind appear to have occurred
in cultures dominated by cities in heterogenetic transformation.
Apart from Rome of the third to the fifth centuries A. D., one might
mention Constantinople from the middle of the 12th to the middle
of the 15th centuries, or the cities of the Iberian peninsula in the
17th and 18th centuries. In both civilizations the decline set in
after contact with other cultures had been made and after the cities
had become centers inhabited by very mixed populations.

On the basis of this reasoning we may draw a number of
conclusions, which form a bridge to the second major problem, the
general theory of urbanization in its relation to economic development and cultural change. The most important phase of the history
of a city from the point of view of its impact on economic growth is
its phase of cultural heterogeneity. In this phase, a city most often
exerts a generative impact on the economic growth of the region it
dominates. Concrete instances of this process have been cited by
Lampard, Kolb, and Davis and Hertz, and they need not be repeated
here. But in some cases a culturally heterogenetic city may exert
a parasitic impact on economic growth, and this impact may either
be of short or long duration. An important question to resolve is
whether we can indicate the variables which determine whether a
culturally heterogenetic city will have a generative or a parasitic
impact.

A further point which results from the preceding discussion is that
the generative or parasitic quality of a city must not be judged with
references to economic growth within the city and its immediate

environs, but only with reference to the wider region which the city dominates. This implies that we assume the relation between a city and the region in which it is located to be one of urban dominance over the rural parts of the region. Whether or not such dominance exists, and which city among several tends to predominate above the others, may be ascertained by the application to concrete cases of the theories of urban hierarchy to which Vining refers. Although Vining, as well as the two urban geographers he cites, Walter Christaller and John E. Brush, are concerned primarily with economic dominance, cultural and political dominance by a city might be exerted along similar lines. Patterns of cultural and political dominance may differ from patterns of economic dominance. For example, in Renaissance Italy the cultural dominance of Florence was not matched by its political importance in relation to other Italian cities; similarly in the United States, Washington has supreme political dominance, but is not dominant from either the economic or cultural viewpoint; at the same time, Detroit and Chicago are economically dominant, but inferior in terms of cultural dominance to Boston and Los Angeles. On the other hand, there are countries in which a city at one and the same time has political, cultural, and economic dominance. Paris, Prague, Athens, Bangkok, Copenhagen, Oslo, Budapest, and many other cities are examples.

A city usually thus exerts dominance over a larger or smaller territory in which it is located, and dominance patterns vary depending upon whether we are concerned with economic, cultural, or political influence. The resultant of these partially overlapping and partially extrinsic fields of dominance appears to be a factor influencing the generative or parasitic impact exercised by a culturally heterogenetic urban center. In the case of colonial administrative centers, which we found to be often parasitic in the short run, the explanation of this outcome lies in the fact that the colonial capital is politically and sometimes culturally dominant within the colony, but economically subordinate to the metropolis. This is true not only of colonial capitals in the narrow sense of the term but often even of cities which have an analogous position to colonial capitals, but which are located in politically independent countries. Montevideo, Panama, or Caracas are politically dominant in the countries of which they are the capitals. But they are economically subordinate to the great centers of world trade for which they are the gateways to the hinterland which they dominate. This tends to produce parasitic features in these cities which at times may overbalance the generative features they normally would be expected to display.

This dichotomy between cultural-political dominance, on the one hand, and economic subordination to external centers, on the other, appears also to have been at the basis of the parasitic role of cities like late medieval Constantinople and seventeenth century Lisbon. Constantinople's economic subordination under Venice during the last three centuries of the Byzantine Empire is too well known to need repetition. Similarly Lisbon in the period after the loss of Portuguese independence came under the economic dominance first of Spain and later of Britain.

These cities occupy a Janus-faced position with regard to the regions within which they have cultural and political dominance, but whose economic subordination they represent at the same time. Further light on their parasitism is thrown by the presence at the same time of different social-structural variables in their economic and cultural-political relations. Kolb has shown that the formation of the western city, of which Chicago was chosen as the prototype, was associated with a transformation of a particularistic-ascriptive value orientation to an universalistic-achievement oriented one.

He also argues that the process of urbanization in underdeveloped countries, in order to be successful, must follow a similar pattern. This argument is in agreement with views I expressed in a recent article on the social-structural change associated with a transition from economic underdevelopment to economic advancement. However, I confined by analysis there only to "those sets of action systems which pertain to a description of economically relevant behavior, i.e., behavior related to the production and distribution of goods and services (4)." Moreover, I included in the analysis not merely the ascription-achievement and the universalism-particularism dichotomies but also a consideration of the other three pairs of pattern variables stipulated by Parsons, particularly the specificity-diffuseness dichotomy. This last pair of variables is stressed by Lampard in his analysis of division of labor and increasing specialization. Its addition appears to me important because, in general, there exists a close functional correlation between ascription, particularism, and functional diffuseness on the one hand, and achievement, universalism, and functional specificity, on the other. But although such a close functional relation between each pair of pattern variables may be stipulated for a given area of social action, e.g., economic activity or political activity, it is not necessary that in the same society all fields of social action display the same structural variables. It is conceivable that economic relations, for example, are ruled by principles of achievement, universalism, and functional specificity, but that political relations display the principles of ascription, particularism, and functional diffuseness.

Differences such as these appear to account for the more or less permanent parasitism of certain cities. In its domestic environment, in the cultural-political order, the city is governed by principles of ascription and particularism; in its economic relations, which are dominated by strangers, achievement, universalism, and functional specificity dominate, or at least are in the ascendancy. The conflict between these two principles in different spheres of social life and action may produce incongruences which we describe as parasitism. The difference between long-run and short-run parasitism with regard to economic growth results from the preponderance of either the economic or the cultural-political relations in a given city. If there is reason to assume that the more "modern and rational," i. e., universalistic-achievement oriented tendencies of economic action are likely to prevail, the city's parasitism may be expected to change over into a state of generativeness. If, on the other hand, cultural-political resistances, the domination of vested interests, or the rigidity of a "great tradition" on the defensive, predominate, we may expect parasitism with regard to economic growth in the long run. In this situation only a revolutionary change in the political or cultural order of the city may end its parasitic role.

This discussion has led us already some distance into the field of a general theory of the relations between urbanization, economic growth, and cultural change. It is not necessary to point out that we cannot boast of possessing a full theory, and that even those theoretical propositions which are summarized here, and which appear in the other papers submitted to this conference would still require a considerable amount of empirical support in order to be conclusively verified.

In this task one must distinguish three cases which are related to one another but may be analyzed separately: I. The problem of economic growth and cultural change within a city; II. the relation between a city's economic growth and cultural change and associated development in the region in which the city is dominant; and III. the problem of economic development and cultural change of a country mediated through the development of a system of urban places, which come to form the urban hierarchy in the country in process of change. The papers of Lampard and Kolb as well as a substantial portion of the paper of Redfield and Singer are directed to the first problem. Similarly, the theoretical summary in the paper by Davis and Hertz centers on the first problem, although some comments of the second are included. Vining's paper deals primarily with the third problem, whereas some of the comments made in the preceding pages of this paper relate primarily to the second problem.

In summarizing the entire discussion it may perhaps be useful to state the agreements and disagreements in terms of these three cases. This may provide us with a rough guide as to where there are still gaps and lacunae in our theoretical framework, and it may also point to those portions of our theory which need refinement, further verification, or revision.

As concerns the first problem, economic growth and cultural change within the confines of the city and its immediate environs, we may attain a fairly complete theory if we combine the propositions of Lampard and Davis and Hertz about economic change (spatial concentration of production; specialization of productive tasks; external economies due to geographical propinquity; availability of a trained labor force and of social overhead; favorable conditions for the development of tertiary industries) with those of Redfield and Singer about cultural change (cities of heterogenetic transformation, with special emphasis on the patterns of cultural change in "metropolis-cities of the world-wide managerial and entrepreneurial class"; rise of a consensus based on self-interest and pecuniary calculation, i. e., a consensus appropriate to the modern, Western technical order;

evolution of sentiments of common cause attached to groups drawn from culturally heterogenous backgrounds; emphasis on prospective rather than retrospective view of man in the universe) and with those of Kolb on changes in social structure (development of universalistic-achievement oriented values and all that implies). Social structure and economic activity may be related by clarifying the connections between an universalistic-achievement oriented society and a culture which places emphasis on a prospective rather than retrospective view of man and in which consensus appropriate to a rationalized technical-economic order is achieved.

This framework describes in the most general terms the relations between the process of economic development and cultural change and the growth and development of a city. There is, however, one caution which should be exercised. Redfield and Singer mention as a special case the "colonial" cities, and ask whether they can reverse from the heterogenetic to the orthogenetic transformation. They conclude that such a development is unlikely. Since these cities do not display a clearly dominant cultural pattern, we may ask further whether the "normal" development described in the preceding paragraph may be expected in them. Redfield and Singer have shown the typical (though not necessarily universal) process of cultural change associated with economic development to be from primary to secondary urbanization. But primary urbanization normally implies the development of a strong, dominant, integrated culture within a city, which then becomes modified in the process of heterogenetic cultural transformation. In general this heterogenetic transformation consists in an accommodation of new culture elements into the dominant culture. The development of the economy of the city is made possible without an excessive degree of social disorganization because, and to the extent to which, the dominant culture of the city is flexible enough to permit a more or less gradual and "orderly" introduction of new culture elements. Kolb has shown how strong may be the forces making for social disorganization and how powerful must be the cultural restraints in order to prevent rapid economic development from creating social chaos and thus defeating itself, in the long run.

In many "colonial" cities a strong, dominant, integrated culture is absent. In addition, the recent process of urban growth in many of these cities has been marked by the following characteristics: I. It has been unusually rapid (as is shown, for example, by the data for Africa presented by Davis and Hertz). II. It has, in many cases, reinforced the ethnic and cultural heterogeneity of the urban population. III. It has occurred not in response to the availability of economic opportunities, especially employment opportunities, in the cities, but as a result of pushes and pulls created by political and military insecurity in the countryside and "psychic" attractions of city life. IV. It has been concentrated in a few central cities, sometimes at the expense of the growth of other smaller cities. The already existing imbalance in the distribution of urban centers in some colonial or "quasi-colonial" countries has been reinforced. The capitals of these countries have grown relatively faster than other cities and have become, in the words of Mark Jefferson, "primate" cities (5). I shall return to this problem later in the discussion of the relationship between economic development and cultural change and the evolution of an entire urban hierarchy.

If we consider the first three of these factors, especially the second and third, we must conclude that we are facing a phenomenon of urban growth which is somewhat unique. It is, of course, true that some primate cities in Europe reached rather large size before the widespread introduction of industry. For example, Paris had some

750,000 inhabitants around the year 1700, and several other European capitals were not very much behind even though their degree of industrialization was of subordinate magnitude(6). But the most rapid period of growth of European cities falls in the period of the industrialization of the various countries, and, as Lampard shows, there was an intimate connection between the economic demands for labor exerted by progressive accumulation of capital in urban industry and the growth of urban centers. This peculiar condition is absent in many of the primate cities of underdeveloped countries in Asia, Africa, and Latin America. Migration to cities takes place for a number of reasons. In part, it is caused by the destruction of the permanent basis for existence in the traditional surroundings of the migrants. In some cases population pressure in the farming regions may become so strong that emigration is necessary for mutual survival, and in other, more frequent cases, peasants are deprived of their traditional livelihood from tillage because of military insecurity, warfare, dacoity, banditry, and other forms of violence. In part the migration to cities is, however, due to pulls exerted by urban conditions. The relatively strong pull of superior consumption patterns has often been noted, and the very low living standards prevailing in most rural areas of underdeveloped countries, coupled with the drabness and the hardships of agricultural labor under conditions of backward technology, makes life in the city appear attractive. It is granted that there are compensations in rural regions, which counterbalance some of these relative disadvantages, but the loosening of cultural restraints as a consequence of inroads made by a more advanced economy, by warfare and political unrest, and a partial breakdown of the traditional kinship ties, create a climate facilitating geographical mobility of persons and their gradual congregation in the primate cities and a few other urban centers.

In spite of the development of intense nationalistic sentiments in some underdeveloped countries, the recent rapid growth of their capitals continues to exhibit culturally heterogenetic features. Migrants to the cities come from the various cultures indigenous to the underdeveloped country rather than from foreign countries. But the cultural heterogeneity of a city like Rangoon is not much diminished if instead of a mixture of Burmans, Indians, and Britishers, the mixture is one of Burmans, Karens, Shans, and Chins. Moreover, the agglomeration of the population occurs on the grounds of economically "irrational" motivations. It is provoked not by an increasing demand for labor in urban centers, but rather by considerations outside the sphere of resource allocation and use.

The combined impact of these factors is likely to prevent the smooth development of a universalist-achievement oriented value structure. To the extent to which tendencies for its development have been present in colonial and "quasi-colonial" capitals, they have been fostered by the dominant influence of Europeans and have perhaps been reinforced by the characteristics of these cities as exclaves in their countries. To the extent to which the attainment of independence and the rise of nationalism tend to destroy or diminish this European influence, the main cultural group favoring the development of universalist-achievement oriented values becomes pushed into a subordinate position. At the same time, there is nothing to take its place, for the "impersonal forces of the market" which were a characteristic aspect of European capitalism and one of the main forces favoring the development of these values are operating only haltingly and imperfectly in the primate cities of underdeveloped countries. Their operation is, moreover, concentrated in those activities which are oriented towards the world markets rather than the domestic labor market, or even the domestic commodity markets.

The prospective socio-economic development of the cities in underdeveloped countries may, therefore, not follow the pattern of development exhibited by cities in advanced Western countries. Kolb recognizes this when he suggests than an alternative pattern prevailing there may be based on universalistic-ascriptive orientations. In view of the development of cultural heterogeneity in these cities which is characterized not any more by a contrast of a dominant European to a submerged native culture, but rather by a diversity of value orientations based only in part on ethnic disparity and to an increasing degree on social differentiation, particularism, rather than universalism, may play an important role.

Let us take another look at Rangoon is order to clarify this statement. Before independence, the characteristic mark impressed upon Rangoon was the dominance of Europeans. This dominance was exerted primarily by the fact that Rangoon's major function was that of a part through which the products of Burma passed into the world markets and through which, at the same time, the products of the world market entered Burma. Rangoon was, therefore, the main locus at which the culture of Burma became affected and modified by that of the West. Economically Westerners were dominant, and even in the second rank of economic dominance we find Indians (culturally more adjusted to the West than the native Burmese). Moreover, even among the Burmese preference was given to those who adopted certain Western cultural values, such as Christianity. The cultural heterogeneity of Rangoon can be described as exhibiting the impact of Western culture on the native culture of Burma and the modifications occurring in this culture provoked by the economic dominance of Westerners. The greater economic "success" of the West was the means by which the cultural impact was primarily exerted. This preponderance of the economic factor (which has led, among

others, to Boeke's well-known theory of the dual economy) (7)
made Rangoon an exclave of Burma. It existed as one of the emporia
of the world market rather than as a capital of a native, culturally
distinct, population.

After independence this situation changed. Rangoon's economic
position with regard to the world market became altered relatively
little. But the internal relationship between the dominance of
Rangoon's economic function and its cultural function as a center
of a native culture became reversed. Although it remains the
gate through which the foreign trade of Burma passes, this function is now subordinated to Rangoon's function as the capital of an
independent country with its own culture. But Burmese society is
not homogeneous. It is linguistically and culturally heterogeneous
and the distinctions between Burmans, Karens, Shans, and Chins
are not confined to culture but extend to the social-political level.
Whereas a society with a "dual economy" exhibited fairly clear-cut
distinctions, and a relatively unambituous pattern of dominance and
subordination, the "plural society, " which replaced it, is in many
ways more complex and dominance patterns vary as between different areas of social action. Though the Burmans may hold a monopoly of political power, Karens exert greater economic power in some
fields, and European and Indian influences are not eradicated in certain intellectual milieus. The Burman elite itself is not and cannot
be culturally "pure. " The consequence of this situation appears to
be a reinforcement of particularistic values (8). Hence the problem
of the prospective development of cities in underdeveloped countries
is not yet fully clear and it appears that here is an important further
problem for research.

The development may lead toward a universalist-achievement
oriented value structure and some cities in underdeveloped countries

could be mentioned which apparently provide examples for this
alternative. São Paulo, Caracas, and some other cities, especially
in Latin America, belong in this group. The development may lead
also to the predominance of particularistic-achievement oriented
values, and some of the capitals of South Asian nations, Colombo,
Rangoon, Jakarta, and others -- as well as the cities in India, if
Marriott's analysis is accepted -- fall into this group. Finally,
we may have the development of universalist-ascription oriented
values, and these may be the patterns of urban growth in China.
Some cities in underdeveloped countries may, moreover, exhibit
several of these features simultaneously. This represents a
transitional stage the general outcome of which is as yet uncertain.

I now wish to turn shortly to a discussion of the problem of the
relation between economic growth and cultural change within the
city and the associated development of the region in which the city
is dominant. So far I have tacitly assumed that the impact is essentially a one-way process, that change occurs in the city and is
transmitted to the surrounding countryside. This uniformity is
questioned, and in my opinion, rightly so, by Redfield and Singer.
The obvious exception which they cite is the process of primary
urbanization. But apart from this instance, which we will disregard
here because we are concentrating only on situations of cultural
heterogeneity, they suggest that the process of mutual cultural interaction between the city and the country needs further exploration.
Here is a problem which is, as yet, very little studied and which
would require the formulation of some testable hypotheses. Most
of the methods which have been developed to study the interrelations
between city and country have been based on several implicit assumptions. One of these has been that of the cultural dominance of
the city. This is exhibited by the very ingenious devices developed

by urban geographers and social ecologists who analyzed the urban hierarchy or the sociology of urban centers (9). Other characteristics of these methods are that they are essentially static, i.e., relate to the description of a situation at one point in time, rather than to a process, and that they concentrate almost exclusively upon the economic functions of the city. Both of these characteristics as well as the assumption of urban dominance are displayed also in Bogue's work on metropolitan communities (10). In fact, as the subtitle of Bogue's work indicates, he is concerned essentially with the patterns of urban dominance, and, as his work shows, this pattern of dominance is exhibited particularly in the economic relations of cities. It is perhaps no accident that Bogue can discern patterns of urban dominance so clearly in the United States. This is the country with the most highly developed economy. It is sometimes said that in the United States urban culture has penetrated into the most remote spots of the countryside. But its high degree of economic development also implies a high degree of economic interdependence, and for this reason economic factors may be used with greater advantage than others as indicators of the closeness or remoteness of relations between population centers and surrounding areas. Bogue's scheme of dominance is, therefore, entirely based on the economic relations between cities and their less densely populated hinterlands. Although some of the other schema developed to describe patterns of urban hierarchy are not as rigidly tied to economic relations as Bogue's model, they rarely include any measures which clearly fall into the realm of cultural contacts. It is true that such measures as newspaper readership are sometimes added, or that -- as is done, for example, by Christaller -- certain political or administrative factors are included, but the most important variables which these models include are economic indicators.

This means that even to the extent to which static models of the mutual impact between cities and their wider hinterland exist, only a partial set of factors relevant for this interdependence have so far been examined, and it would be desirable to develop methods which would take account of non-economic factors. I have no doubt that this would be an extremely difficult procedure, and that it would be especially difficult to find variables which could be subjected to quantitative analysis as easily as can many economic variables. At the same time, it might be possible to obtain some more light on this mutual interdependence in areas of non-economic activity if such factors as linguistic and ethnic differences in cities and their hinterlands, perhaps membership in religious organizations and intensity of religious activities, length and purposes of seasonal migrations and travel, were studied. Which of these (or any other) factors should receive prominence would depend on the development of a theoretical framework of cultural dynamics and this is, alas, still lacking in most of its essential portions.

The fact that most existing models of the interrelations between cities and their hinterlands are static is of less concern. It is, of course, granted that what we are interested in chiefly is an analysis of the process of cultural change and economic growth. But this does not mean that this process can be studied only by applying dynamic models. As a first approximation the method of comparative statics may be used. In other words, the process of cultural change and related economic development and their interrelations with the process of urbanization may be adequately explored by attempting to find functional relationships between these variables and subvariables and by comparing static situations which are related to one another through time. Here the contribution of the historical study of urbanization may be most important. But in order to obtain results

about the relationship of cities to their hinterlands, the historical
study of cities must free itself from concentrating on urban history
in the narrow sense and must expand into a study of the historical
dimension of city-country interdependence and interrelations.
Again I am ready to acknowledge that it is not easy to state in
specific terms the concrete formulation of problems which may
be expected to yield meaningful research results. But I hope that
a recognition of this problem may lead to such formulation and to
the discovery of appropriate methods by which answers to the kinds
of questions posed here may be found.

The third problem area is the determination of relationships
between economic growth and cultural change and the development
not of one city but an entire net of cities which stand in some order
of hierarchy to one another. This problem is treated explicitly by
Vining though it is dealt with, by implication, also by the authors of
all the other papers. The first comment which may be made here,
and which follows from much of what has been said earlier in this
paper, is that the "system of cities" as described by Vining, in which
cities if ordered by rank and size are distributed in accordance with
Pareto's law, seems to hold only for countries with a relatively high
degree of industrialization. In the industrially less developed countries,
the "law of primate cities" in its more extreme form appears to hold.
In fact, in some underdeveloped countries this "law of the primate
city" is so strong that apart from a capital which may have a million
inhabitants or more, there are no other "large" cities, i.e., cities
of more than 100,000 inhabitants. Perhaps the two most outstanding
examples are Thailand and Peru (11). In each the metropolitan city
(with environs) has a population of around a million and the country
lacks any other urban region exceeding 100,000 inhabitants. Yet
Thailand has a population of more than eighteen and Peru of almost

ten million. In some other less developed countries the predominance of the capital is not so pronounced, but the over-all disproportions between the largest, the small group of large, and the mass of small and minute cities is also sufficiently pronounced so as to make the rank-size rule inapplicable. This extreme degree or urban concentration in relatively few centers can be found not only in many underdeveloped countries, but also in many European countries before the industrial revolution. The pre-eminence of Paris at the time of Louis XIV has already been mentioned. It should be added, however, that at the time Paris had several hundred thousand inhabitants, there was no other French city which even reached 100,000. The same was true of Britain. At the time of the Glorious Revolution, London had around 700,000 inhabitants, and Bristol, the second city in Great Britain at that date, only around 50,000 (12).

If Vining is correct in his statement that a Pareto distribution holds in all "developed systems of cities," and that in the United States this size-rank distribution has "maintained a fairly stable form since 1790," we are faced with two problems: I. The development of a system of cities in the United States -- perhaps as a consequence of its rapid settlement -- has been unusual and it is, therefore, perhaps not proper to draw inferences from its past development to what may happen in presently underdeveloped countries, especially those which are more densely populated now than the United States was before the middle of the 19th century. II. The present system of cities in the United States is characteristic of a "developed" system of cities. If countries of reasonably sizeable population are found in which this relationship does not hold, can we infer that these countries have an "underdeveloped" system of cities? And if so, what are the characteristics of an

"underdeveloped" system of cities? In France and Britain the
relative preponderance of the capital is still very pronounced, in
spite of the relatively high level of economic development which
these two countries exhibit. In France, especially, the rank-size
rule does not fit well. It would be approximated much better if the
agglomeration of Paris were left out of the picture. But Paris
cannot be left out of the picture -- not only because without Paris,
France would not be France -- but rather because France exhibits,
in spite of industrialization and economic growth, the pattern of
predominance of a primate city. This means that even granting
the general applicability of the rank-size rule to a system of cities
in an economically developed country, we are left with the problem
of determining what distortions of this rule are caused by cultural
and political factors, the differences between trends towards
political centralization as against federalism, the historical
patterns of settlement of a country, and, in the last resort, its
entire demographic and economic history.

What I am trying to say is that the apparently neat and simple
relationship that can be stipulated -- in a rough way -- for the
system of cities of some countries, may become strongly modified
if other, especially non-economic, factors are introduced. Depending upon whether the factors accounting for the deviation of
any actual distribution from the theoretically postulated one are
all outside the realm of economic relations or not, it will become
possible to predict with a somewhat higher degree of dependability
how and in what ways economic growth and a rank-size distributed
system of cities are related. I fear that some of the factors determining the deviations are economic, or at least demographic-
historical factors, and hence any close correlation between the
level of economic development and a particular pattern of distribution of urban centers may never be established.

Although some of these factors may be of importance with reference to the problem in which we are here primarily interested, the most important query that arises, if one considers the usefulness of such models for the study of economic development and cultural change, is the meaning of the function of the various central places in the model. The list of service functions in Wisconsin hamlets, villages and towns, which Vining cites from Brush, exhibit characteristic aspects of a highly developed economy. A similar list of hamlets, villages and towns in an underdeveloped country, say India, would show a very different set of typical functions of each central place of a given order. Whether a theory of central places can be applied to our problem depends, therefore, not so much on the presence or absence of regularities in locational patterns, but rather on whether we can compare meaningfully central places of different order in countries on different levels of economic development. Moreover, since cultural factors affect the functions of cities, differences in culture would add another element possibly still further limiting comparability. Yet, it is probable that an urban hierarchy analogous to that in southern Germany or Wisconsin exists in underdeveloped countries, especially those with many central places. The higher-order central places would probably be more similar in their service functions to one another in countries with different levels of economic development than central places of lower order. For example, a city like Bombay or Madras would differ less (in significant service functions) from Chicago or Milwaukee than some Indian small town of 10,000 inhabitants from Baraboo or Prairie du Chien, Wisconsin. At the same time, it is doubtful whether in Wisconsin, or the entire United States, central places could be found which correspond in function to Benares or Mecca.

Since the characteristics of central places of different order are derived primarily from economic functions, those central places in underdeveloped countries which in their economic structure most resemble corresponding central places in more developed countries would show the greatest functional similarities. This is true primarily of the large cities, especially those which in the colonial and ex-colonial countries form exclaves, i.e., in their primary function, are appendages of the system of world markets. But the cult places, as well as those central places in underdeveloped countries in which assimilation to Western culture has progressed the least, would show much greater functional differences with corresponding central places in Western countries. A comparative analysis of central places might show therefore the degree to which a rationalized Western system of economic organization and activity has penetrated a given country and might be a fairly good measure of the breadth on which the economic development of a country has taken place. Here again, cultural differences and historical traditions would blur the picture and introduce deviations which would have to be specially accounted for in each case.

All these procedures, however, only provide yardsticks for comparison, approximations of stages of economic development, and criteria for classification. They would have to be supplemented by a theory in which the development of a given system of cities is related to processes of economic growth. Such a theory is as yet non-existent, but it is possible that further study and refinement of some of the relations studied by the protagonists of urban hierarchy or the theorists of systems of cities may lead to one. Here then is a field in which research has just begun and has therefore progressed very little. It presents perhaps a greater challenge and offers a wider scope for research than almost any problem area discussed so far.

It appears as if we had come a long way from our original problem, the distinction between generative and parasitic roles of cities, but in truth, the propositions discussed in the previous paragraphs are alternative statements of this problem, especially if we consider that the question of whether and under what circumstances cities exert a generative or a parasitic impact is an alternative way of asking what are the general relations between the processes of economic growth and cultural change on the one hand, and urbanization on the other. Depending upon whether we focus on these processes within a city, in the city's hinterland, or in an entire country undergoing a process of development accompanied by the formation of a net of urban centers, we encounter different sub-problems and may come out with different evaluations of the generativeness or the parasitism of a given city or set of cities.

The over-all process of development of a system of cities corresponding more or less to the functional and size distribution presented by Vining may be considered as the most general pattern of economic development in which urbanization plays a predominantly generative role. To the extent to which this development of a system of cities is impeded, or to the extent to which a top-heavy system exhibiting the characteristics of primate-city domination cannot be overcome (and especially in those cases where the dominance of a primate city is reinforced in the process of urbanization), we may find a series of at least temporary parasitic influences exerted by the primate city. The particular form of this parasitism as well as the seriousness and duration of its impact will depend, as I believe to have shown, upon the particular constellation of economic and non-economic (primarily cultural, political, and social-structural) factors. The determination of these factors, and of their interrelations, becomes then one of the primary research tasks in the study of the mutual interrelation between urbanization and economic development and cultural change.

NOTES TO CHAPTER VIII

* This essay was written originally as a summary of a Conference on the Role of Cities in Economic Development, held in Chicago in May, 1954. The other paper presented at the Conference to which reference is made in the text were published in Nos. 1 and 2 of Volume III (October, 1954 and January 1955) of Economic Development and Cultural Change.

1. Colin Clark, The Conditions of Economic Progress, 2nd ed. (London, 1951).

2. For a description of this process in Strassburg, for example, see Gustav Schmoller, Strassburgs Blüte und die volkswirtschaftliche Revolution im XIII Jahrhundert (Strassburg, 1875), pp. 11 ff.; the same development in 13th and early 14th century Geneva has been described by Francis de Crue, La guerre féodale de Genève et l'establissement de la commune (1285-1320) (Geneva, 1907).

3. On the early history of Batavia and its impact, see for example, J. J. Van Klaveren, The Dutch Colonial System in the East Indies (Rotterdam, 1953), pp. 40 ff.

4. See Chapter II. above.

5. Mark Jefferson, "The Law of the Primate City," Geographical Review, Vol. 29, No. 2 (April 1939), pp. 226-232.

6. See Emile Levasseur, La population française (Paris, 1889), I, p. 213.

7. See J. H. Boeke, The Structure of the Netherlands Indian Economy (New York), 1942, Ch. I.

8. McKim Marriott arrives at a similar conclusion by a somewhat different process of reasoning.

9. A good review of some of the most recent literature is presented by John E. Brush, "The Urban Hierarchy in Europe," Geographical Review, Vol. 43, No. 3 (July 1953), pp. 414-416.

10. Donald J. Bogue, The Structure of the Metropolitan Community: A Study in Dominance and Subdominance (Ann Arbor, 1950).

11. For further examples, see Jefferson, op. cit.

12. These data are based on the estimate of Sir William Petty, "Essays in Political Arithmetic," in Tracts (Dublin, 1759), pp. 182 ff.

9

URBANIZATION AND ECONOMIC
GROWTH IN ASIA

I

Few social institutions have received such contradictory
evaluations as cities. On the one hand they are represented as the
source of all moral evils and physical degradations which mankind
has suffered. On the other hand they are painted as the glory of
civilization and the zenith of human achievement in the co-ordinated
use of space. These judgments are pronounced, not merely by posts
or nature enthusiasts, but by philosophers and students of social
relations. How can they be reconciled, and what is the true role
cities have played in the unfolding of civilization? More specifically, what was the place of urban development in the growth of
the highly complex and productive economies of the western world,
and in what way can or must these experiences be repeated if the
present underdeveloped countries are to attain levels of material
welfare commensurate with those of the more advanced countries?

These are big questions, and I cannot hope to answer them in the
short space at my disposal. But I should like to set down, in outline, some considerations on the relationship between the growth
of cities and economic growth. This relationship appears obvious
at first sight, since the most highly developed countries are also,
on the whole, most highly urbanized. The rapid growth of urban
centers in Europe, moreover, set in approximately at the same time

217

as the first steps toward rapid industrialization were taken. Since that time, industrialization and urbanization have been regarded as closely related processes. The presence of large cities and, indeed, of systems of cities is made by some a measure of the degree of economic "maturity" of a country, and this view implies that not merely urbanization as such but a particular pattern of urbanization is associated with economic growth.

Up to the recent past, the reasons for and against these propositions have been discussed little, and even at present a rigorous theoretical analysis of the association between economic growth and urbanization is lacking. But the question may be raised whether there exists a necessary strict correlation between these two processes, whether industrial growth cannot take place by a process of planned decentralization, and whether, on the other hand, urbanization is a phenomenon which appears even without concomitant industrialization. With our present knowledge, any generalization about the association between urbanization and economic growth is based not on any well-established social theory, but merely upon their joint historical occurrence. For this reason, we may trace through the role and functions that cities may play in economic development and determine the extent to which a process of economic growth may be dependent upon urbanization. At the same time, we may ask what are the costs of urbanization, and how heavily does the development of cities draw upon productive resources which, in the absence of urban growth, might be used for capital formation furthering the productive attainments of a society.

An analysis of the relationship between urbanization and economic growth may start either with an historical description of the development of cities or with a distinction of the functional characteristics of cities and the relative frequency with which cities of a certain type appear in countries at different levels of economic performance. In distinguishing cities functionally, and even in describing the history of cities, their economic role is usually stressed. Yet it appears that in early times and in economically little advanced societies, the city plays predominantly a non-economic role. Its function is that of a religious or cult center, or a political adminis- trative center, or a central place of protection. It acquires econo- mic functions because it already has religious or political functions and because it is usually built in an easily accessible spot. The city with primarily economic functions is a rather late development. In the Mediterranean basin, two millenia of urban civilization had been in existence before the first trading colonies -- urban places with primarily economic functions -- were founded by the Phoenicians and Greeks. In medieval Europe we also encounter some urban centers which were simply trade centers and had no other functions at the outset. But in antiquity as in the Middle Ages, the majority of cities developed out of administrative, political, or religious centers and attained their economic functions only later, usually as a consequence of the successful development of these other non-economic functions. And similarly, many cities in non-European civilizations were originally political or cult centers, and acquired important economic functions because they performed successfully their non-economic roles.

The city in which economic considerations are clearly in the foreground is the modern industrial city. Thus, it is quite ap- propriate to classify modern American cities primarily by their predominant economic role (1). To the extent to which western patterns of urban growth and functional specialization have been adopted in non-European countries, the same functional types can be distinguished. Thus we find today mining towns, or manufacturing

towns, or commercial towns in Asia, Africa, and Latin America.
But most of these towns are of recent origin, or have had this
economic characteristic impressed upon them only in the last
few decades, and if we look at the older cities in these parts of
the world, we find that they have an important history as political
or cult centers.

The reason why one must insist on this predominantly non-
economic function of cities in little industrialized countries, and
why one must beware of placing too much emphasis on their economic function is not difficult to see. In societies with little industrialization and a relatively low level of economic performance,
the city has an influence primarily as a center of political and administrative power and a place in which the cultural achievements
of a society are brought to their highest point of elaboration. This
process has been designated by Redfield and Singer as orthogenetic
cultural transformation. It takes place characteristically in cities
which exist in non-industrial environments. Many of the old centers
in Asian countries have been -- and some still are -- cities of
orthogenetic cultural transformation. In many of these cities, new
functions and new tasks have been superimposed, and side by side
with them new cities have been founded which have predominantly
administrative or economic functions. These latter cities have been
described by Redfield and Singer as cities of heterogenetic transformation, and their characteristics are that:

> ...men are concerned with the market, with 'rational' organi-
> zation of production of goods, with expediential relations be-
> tween buyer and seller, ruler and ruled, and native and foreigner.
> In this kind of city the predominant social types are business-
> men, administrators alien to those they administer, and rebels,
> reformers, planners, and plotters of many varieties (2).

The dichotomy between orthogenetic and heterogenetic transformation which is implied in this schema must be regarded as a postulate

of two extreme ideal types, and the actual features of cities in western countries and in Asia and Africa fall somewhere in between. To some extent, all or almost all cities have contributed to the intellectual development of the societies in which they were located, and perhaps only those towns which arose in the early industrial age in Europe and America, and which Lewis Mumford has called the "insensate industrial towns" come close to representing the heterogenetic form in a fairly pure style (3). But these cities with exclusive economic functions exist only in countries in which economic development has attained already a relatively high degree, and although there are some signs that a few cities of this kind may be evolving in underdeveloped countries, they are as yet little numerous there, and policies may be devised and brought to bear avoiding the repetition of the growth of these "insensate" industrial towns in more newly urbanized countries.

The overwhelming majority of cities, especially of large cities, in underdeveloped countries, have multiple functions. To be sure, in some, the commercial or industrial functions stand out, but most of them are, at the same time, centers of government and intellectual life. If there are significant differences between the large cities of Asia and Africa, on the one hand, and those of Europe, on the other, they derive from the fact that non-European cities are, on the whole, younger than those of Europe, and that the urban populations of Europe have developed a more pronounced "urban consciousness" than those of non-European countries. This weakness of urban consciousness in Asia and Africa is in turn an outflow of the relative recency of growth of non-European cities, but, in a more profound sense, it is tied to differences in the nature of urban institutions in the Orient and the West. The main institutional feature of the European city, which has been stressed above all by Max Weber, is its autonomous corporate character.

Weber admitted freely that in terms of density of settlement and
specialization of economic function, the Orient knew places which
were "cities." He also admitted that outside the western world, cities
existed in the sense of fortified points or seats of political or religious
administration. But only in the Occident did there develop the concept
of a city as a unitary community. In the Middle Ages, its distinguishing
mark was the possession of its own law, court, and autonomous administration. The citizen of the Middle Ages was a citizen insofar as
he came under this law and participated in the choice of administrative
officials. The origin of the European city as a community of defense,
an economic entity, and a federation based on common participation in
religious ritual, is well described by Weber and requires no further
discussion here. But this original coniuratio on which city status in
Europe is based, and which made anyone eligible for membership in
the city who by religion or servile status was not excluded from participating in this common oath, forms the bedrock of a tradition of
urban consciousness which has remained alive all over Western
Europe and has been transplanted to those overseas territories which
are inhabited by populations having their origin in Western Europe (4).

The practical significance of this difference in "urban consciousness"
is its impact upon the stability and progress of urban institutions in
European and non-European countries. It may, in the last resort, be
one of the reasons why some past effects of European cities in furthering
a more uniform cultural expression will be modified to some extent in
Asia and Africa, and why patterns of industrialization may well take on
different forms in Asia from those they have embraced in Europe and
North America.

II

These observations must serve as an introduction, setting the stage
for our investigation of the role of cities in the economic development

of Asian countries. The problem we are confronted with there appears to be the following: the cities, especially the capital cities and other large centers, are on the whole new settlements. They often were founded by outsiders (e.g., Djakarta or Karachi), and their growth has been influenced largely by their situation close to the sea and their being the main gateways of international and interregional trade. Since the end of the war, these cities have experienced a rapid rate of growth and have tended to assemble vast populations for whom neither employment nor housing and other facilities were available. South Asia thus has been described as "over-urbanized" at the present state.

The recency of the foundation and growth, the absence of a tradition of urban consciousness in Asian and African cities, and the heterogeneity of urban populations have imposed serious strains. Poverty and crime, the absence of decent standards of housing, hygiene, recreational facilities, and other amenities are reported from the cities of all underdeveloped countries, and the incidence of slums and other signs of destitution is widespread.

These factors impinge upon the economic role of cities in South Asia. In terms of traditional cost-benefit analysis, the non-measurable costs -- represented by these forms of social disorganization -- are vast, and for cities to have, on the whole, a favorable effect on economic growth, their measurable and non-measurable benefits must be even vaster. It may well turn out that urbanization in Asia is proceeding at too rapid a rate, and that urban populations tend to be too heavily concentrated in a few primate cities. Yet this urban growth and even the high degree of concentration may be a necessary concomitant of social and intellectual progress. Since education is one of the most important means of improving economic performance in underdeveloped countries, the impact of cities upon the level and kind

of educational facilities is of the greatest importance. And it is in
this context that primate cities play an important role. For although
the primate city imposes heavier social costs because of its large
size, it also exerts a more profound and more lasting effect upon
changing patterns of social behavior. In the primate cities of Asia
which are seats of governments of new independent countries, the
intellectual and political as well as the economic and communications
elites have their headquarters. There new ideas of government and
economic policy are evolved and shaped and development plans designed
and implemented. Moreover, the primate cities in Asia are the
most important centers of cultural change, especially in those fields
which vitally affect economic development. Advanced education, new
forms of business organization, new administrative practices, and,
last but not least, new technologies find a fertile soil in these primate
capital cities. Their intermediate position between East and West,
their contact with world markets of commodities and ideas, their
lack of many traditional bonds make them into eminently suitable
vehicles for the introduction of new ideas and new techniques. If
economic development is associated with modernization, the mediation
of new, "more modern" forms of social action through the primate
cities of Asia is an indispensable part of this process (5).

Thus the picture we witness in many Asian countries in one which
has no proper analogue in the past urban developments of the West.
Although in preindustrial periods primate cities existed there also,
the overall cultural distance of these cities from the countryside
surrounding them was never as great as in present-day underdeveloped
countries. Although in their settlement patterns, and even in their
overall population composition, the cities of Asia are closer to the
countryside than was the case of European cities, except during short
periods of their history, the cultural distance between city and country-

side is greater in the newly developing countries than in Europe.

The reasons for this contrast between city and country in under-developed countries is, above all, the newness of the cities. Industry has been introduced more recently than in the West. In the countries which were under European colonial rule, many of the cities were founded by colonial officials or traders from Europe, and were administered and governed by members of a European or Europeanized civil service. These cities are "cultural importations" from abroad.

But in addition to their newness and their foreign origin, the cities in underdeveloped countries are entities which are in many other ways very remote from traditional native culture. Their function has been and continues to be to a large extent that of gateways to the outside world. Since they are not clearly separate entities with their own laws and administration, they do not experience an ordered process of gradual incorporation and absorption of cityward migrants. Rather they grew like Topsy. People came, some of them stayed, and others went away again. Even those who stayed often maintained strong ties with the village, family, or region they had come from. The city was not always recognized by the immigrant as his new final home. It was a temporary residence, a place of passage. This has determined the ecological and the social forms of existence which evolved in cities of underdeveloped countries (6).

But, in addition to this unstable floating population, usually at the lower margins of the social scale, the city harbors a more stable population among which professional people, intellectuals, and members of the middle and wealthier strata stand out. These groups differ more from the common man in the countryside, the recent immigrant, and even the ordinary worker in the city than in Western countries. Above all, the economic differences between the two groups are usually greater. Next, differences in political power and social status are usually greater. Finally, differences in culture and world view are greater. If the urban elite is tradition-oriented (i.e., if the city is in the phase of orthogenetic transformation), it is made up of literate priests and aristocrats; if it is a "modernizing" elite (i.e., if the city is in the phase of heterogenetic transformation), its members are western-educated persons who often are far removed in their thinking and action from the less "secularized" and frequently still profoundly tradition-oriented rural masses. This cultural difference causes the greatest divergence between city and country in Asia and Africa; and the recent rapid growth of Asian cities which has brought so many rural people into the few metropolitan primate centers has tended to enhance this difference, especially as between social groups within the city.

This process of growth of urban areas has been speeded up since the end of the war, so that at present the countries of South Asia may be regarded, on the whole, as "over-urbanized." We arrive at such a judgment in spite of the fact that in Asia only one in twelve persons is a city dweller -- as against one in eight in the world as a whole, approximately one in three in North America, and one in five in Europe -- by the following reasoning. In Table IX-1, the proportion of the population in places of 20,000 inhabitants or more and of 100,000 inhabitants or more in several Asian countries is listed. For Asia, as a whole, approximately 13 per cent of the total population is "urban," and more than 8 per cent "metropolitan urban." Now urban populations are characteristically non-agricultural. Of course, industries are not entirely concentrated in cities, and, in fact, there exist a sizeable number of rural cottage industries, as well as a few large-scale plants in the country. Hence, although the proportion of the urban population is only 13 per cent, the proportion of the non-agricultural labor force is roughly 30 per cent. However, at a similar degree

Table IX-1. Total Population and Urban Population of the Countries of the ECAFE Region - 1950

	Total Population 1950 (Thousands)	Population in Places of 20,000 and More		Population in Places of 100,000 and More		Per cent of Urban Population Living in Places of 100,000 and More
		(Thousands)	Per cent of Population	(Thousands)	Per cent of Population	
Hong Kong	2,260	2,124	94.0	2,124	94.0	100.0
Japan	82,900	35,000	42.1	21,222	25.6	60.8
Malaya and Singapore	6,245	1,617	25.9	1,118	17.9	69.1
Korea	29,291	5,557	19.0	3,876	13.2	69.4
Brunei, North Borneo, and Sarawak	956	134	14.0	0	0	0
Philippines	19,881	2,523	12.7	1,013	5.1	40.1
India	358,000	42,960	12.0	23,628	6.6	55.0
Ceylon	7,544	860	11.4	407	5.4	47.3
Burma	18,489	1,850	10.0	924	5.0	50.0
China (incl. Taiwan)	564,477(a)	56,448	10.0	39,515	7.0	70.0
Indonesia	75,500	6,870	9.1	5,285	7.0	76.9
Cambodia, Laos, and Viet-Nam(b)	30,000(a)	2,400	8.0	1,950	6.5	81.2
Pakistan	75,040	5,853	7.8	3,602	4.8	61.5
Thailand	18,488	1,410	7.6	1,227	6.7	88.1
Afghanistan(c)	12,000	540	4.5	204	1.7	37.7
Nepal	7,000(a)	308	4.4	210	3.0	68.1
ECAFE Region	1,308,071	166,494	12.7	106,305	8.1	63.7
Total Asia	1,368,000	179,208	13.1	113,544	8.3	63.3

a. Unofficial estimate

b. Comprising former Annam, Cochin-China, and Tonkin

Source: United Nations, Bureau of Social Affairs, Population Branch, "Demographic Aspects of Urbanization in the ECAFE Region," in Philip Hauser, ed., Urbanization in Asia and The Far East, (Calcutta, 1957), p. 101

of urbanization in the Western countries, the United States (1850's),
France (1860's), Germany (1880's), and Canada (1890's) had roughly
55 per cent of their labor force engaged in non-agricultural occupations (7
  This fact has several consequences. In the first place, it is a sign
that urbanization in Asia has probably run ahead of industrialization,
and the development of administrative and other service occupations
which are characteristically concentrated in cities. In the second place,
it emphasizes the disproportion between the costs of urban growth and
the maintenance of proper facilities for urban dwellers and the earning
capacity of the people congregated in cities. In the third place, it is
evidence that migration to the city is due less to the "pull," i.e., the
attractiveness, which the city exerts, and more to the "push" experienced
in the country. In general the forces which tend to push people out of
rural regions are associated with the increasing difficulty of making a
living there. In Asia many people have drifted into the city because
political insecurity made living in the country impossible or highly
dangerous, or because bandits and insurgents destroyed their homes, thei
land, or their crops. But in some countries which have been spared from
civil war and banditry, the push to the city has been exerted by the inability of a limited agricultural area to support the rapidly rising number
of young people. Rural open or disguised unemployment became so
impelling that the only way of escape was seen in migration to the city.
In many Asian countries the migrants exchanged a precarious existence
in the country for an equally precarious one in the city.
  This tendency to over-urbanization in Asia has also an important
political aspect. Owing to the greater concentration of population, the
higher degree of literacy among urban than country people, and the
propinquity to centers of political decision-making, the urban population
is more deeply involved in politics than the rural population. Moreover,
the greater degree of literacy and the much greater degree of exposure

to mass communication media make urban populations more susceptible to various forms of political propaganda. Thus, at present, the cities of underdeveloped countries, and above all their primate cities, are the centers of nationalist sentiment and political action. But to the extent to which aspirations for economic advancement are not fulfilled or fulfilled only inadequately, urban populations may become a very responsive element for radical propaganda of various sorts and may easily be induced to support forms of totalitarian policies on the left or on the right. In view of the overwhelming political role exercised by the cities in underdeveloped countries and the relative political impotence of the countryside, the present situation of over-urbanization, coupled with the relatively unsatisfactory employment situation among urban dwellers, must be regarded as an important element of potential political and social instability. It goes without saying that this situation is aggravated by the existing international tension between the Free World and the Soviet Bloc, and the apparent competitive struggle for influence among the non-committed countries in Asia and Africa.

I do not propose to dwell further on this problem in this place, except to say that policies devoted to the problem of industrial location and planning for economic development should properly include consideration of this potential instability. Whether or not we can envisage patterns of economic development in Asia along non-totalitarian lines depends not only upon the rate of capital formation and technical innovation, but also on the distribution of new facilities in such a way as to minimize disappointments of aspirations among the politically most active population sectors. In this sense industrialization and other measures of economic development in the cities of Asia and Africa take on not merely an economic but also an eminently political coloration.

III

Before we can enter into a discussion of the policies designed to
meet the objectives of economic advancement and to deal simultaneously
with the problems raised by the urbanization process which has taken
place so far, we must turn to a short consideration of the past economic effects of urban growth in Asia. The outstanding characteristic
distinguishing urban from rural areas in underdeveloped countries is
the occupational structure oriented to non-agricultural activities.
Manufacturing, and even more pronouncedly service industries find
a natural habitat in cities. This differential occupational pattern is
well exhibited by evidence from India, presented in Table IX-2.

Table IX-2. Distribution of Working Population in India, 1951

	Rural		Urban		Total	
	Million	Per cent	Million	Per cent	Million	Per cent
Primary Industry	71.3	84	2.7	15	74.0	72
Secondary Industry	4.8	6	4.4	24	9.2	9
Tertiary Industry	9.1	10	11.1	61	20.2	19
Total	85.2	100	18.2	100	103.4	100

Source: Census of India 1951, Paper No. 3 (1953).

The data presented in this table speak for themselves. They do
not surprise us, and although similar data for most of the other Asian
countries are not available, they may be accepted as fairly representa-
tive of South Asia as a whole. In Africa the proportion of population
engaged in secondary and tertiary industries is, if anything, smaller
than in India and other countries of Asia.

Let us examine the figures for secondary and tertiary industry somewhat more closely. In absolute numbers, employment in manufacturing
and processing was approximately equal in urban and rural areas. But
proportionately a much larger share of the urban population was engaged
in secondary industry. This should not be interpreted to mean that all,
or even most, urban industrial workers were employed in large-scale

industry. On the contrary, the Indian cities -- and those of other Asian countries as well -- have traditionally been the seats of handicraft industries and continue to be so. This means that with the growth of industry, the number of industrial and handicraft workers who work on their own account have also increased, and in many Asian cities the number of salaried and wage workers in service trades and manufacturing does not exceed the number of self-employed persons (8). In other words, the data presented in Table IX-2 must be interpreted in the light of Asian rather than Western conditions. As yet modern forms of industrial and service activities embrace only a relatively small portion of the labor force, and among this almost exclusively of the urban labor force. Almost all of the roughly 14 million persons in rural India who derived their livelihood from other than primary industries were small artisans, peddlers, traders, and the like. But a fair proportion, perhaps half of the roughly 15 million persons engaged in secondary and tertiary industries in the cities of India, also belonged to this same group of small independent craftsmen or shopkeepers.

Although, therefore, there are some important differences in occupational structure and type of employment relations in cities and rural areas, these differences are limited to a portion only of the urban labor force. Thus, in terms of economic patterns of earning a livelihood and spending one's income, a portion of the urban population represents a transitional group between a model characteristic of rural areas and one characteristic of urban areas. Among the factors which contribute to the change in earning and spending patterns is residence in the city itself, as well as change in the job or employment status of the urban dweller. But the cultural, social, and political impact of living in the city has at least an equal impact to that of the change in employment or occupation upon this transformation of a rural tradition-oriented person to an urban secular-oriented one.

This transformation can be well observed if we compare urban and rural earning and spending patterns. Actual empirical data, especially comparative data, are extremely scanty. A survey sponsored by UNESCO in five Asian cities on the Social Implications of Industrialization and Urbanization is a first concerted attempt to provide data of this kind for the countries of Asia. Additional scattered data are available from census reports, some anthropological field studies, and a few special studies by independent researchers (9). On the basis of these sources we might make the following general observations. Earnings of urban workers are, on the whole, higher than those of rural workers. The differential here is chiefly due to the fact that urban and rural workers are employed in different occupations, i.e., the income differentials between urban and rural workers reflect essentially differences between incomes in agriculture and industry. In general, workers' incomes in the larger cities within each country are higher than in the middling or small cities, but this differential probably also reflects differences in industrial structure rather than wage differentials in the same industry or trade. Since workers' incomes are higher in cities than in the country, and since savings patterns as we shall see, vary little between city and country, the expenditures of urban workers are higher than those of rural workers and hence more and larger businesses may be supported in the city. Moreover, in the city most transactions are mediated by money, whereas in the country in many underdeveloped countries there exists as yet a large amount of subsistence farming and of barter exchange.

If urban earnings are, on the whole, higher than rural earnings, this is counterbalanced by some factors which tend to make real living standards in the city and country more equal -- excepting, of course, always a relatively small percentage of middle and upper income families. In the first place, it is likely that the dependency rate among urban income earners is higher than among rural income earners. This situation results from the change in family structure which is associated with the process of urbanization and in which the male head of the household tends to become the only breadwinner. In a city, women have fewer opportunities for sharing in their husbands' work than on the farm, and children remain longer in a dependency status. Secondly, the cost of living is higher in cities than in the country, a fact which is not surprising, since the urban dweller has to pay for the transportation and other services which were performed to bring the objects of his subsistence near to him. Finally, as people remain in the city, their pattern of consumption changes, and many items of consumption which are not consumed in the country -- because they are unavailable there -- are consumed in the city. The UNESCO study on the Social Implications of Industrialization and Urbanization is replete with examples of this changing pattern of consumption. In Bangkok, as well as in Delhi, in Dacca and in Bombay, new commodities become available to the migrant into the city which he never had known or had never been able to obtain (10).

The net effects of the greater dependency rate, the higher cost of living, and the evolution of wants for new types of consumers' goods has the overall effect that, in spite of higher incomes, urban populations are able to save little, and are found to be in debt as often as rural people. For example, Prabhu elicited some information of indebtedness from his sample of 523 respondents in Bombay. 448 only provided information of whether or not they incurred debts in order to send money home to their village, and only 41 per cent of those said that they did not incur debts for this purpose. The need to send money home, is, of course, not the only demand made on the financial resources of the urban wage earner. As has been shown by Prabhu, and

most elaborately by Sovani and his associates in their study on
Poona, the income earned by many persons in a city is often insufficient to support them and their families. Hence they incur
debts, and the actual capacity to save is not substantially higher
among the mass of the urban than the rural population (11). The
Asian city, therefore, has not yet succeeded in attaining one goal
which urbanization usually produces in the long run: the abolition
of mass poverty. Though urban incomes are well above rural incomes in Asia, at least half of the urban population lives on a level
which is scarcely above and often below actual subsistence, i.e., on
a level at which, with given prices, adequate nutritional, clothing,
and housing standards required for sustained health can scarcely be
met. The prevalence of poverty in Asian and African cities exerts
an impact upon the public services which urban administrations cannot supply. If the incomes of city people are low, their taxable capacity is low, and hence the city government cannot acquire large funds
for public works in the city. Thus we find often little support for
streets, parks, hospitals, schools, and recreational facilities in
municipalities in underdeveloped countries. Even such services as
fire and police protection are often deficient and of uncertain quality.
Joseph Froomkin has shown that, even taking account of the lower income levels of urban peoples in underdeveloped countries as compared
with those in economically more advanced countries, the outlays for
municipal services in non-western countries are disappointing (12).
Though some of the shortcomings of municipal budgeting is made up
from the funds of some higher governmental entity -- usually the central government -- actual expenditures for various municipal services,
and especially welfare services, falls far short of existing needs. In
view of the relative lack of fiscal autonomy of most cities in underdeveloped countries, the cities far away from the capital are usually

much worse off in these respects than the capital. Here is another
factor which enhances the tendency toward the formation of primate
cities and reduces, in general, the economic and social impact
which cities, especially those non-metropolitan centers scattered
about the provinces, might exert.

IV

The economic impact of cities, which I have mentioned, consists
primarily in the impact upon changes in the occupational structure
and the pattern of earnings and consumption by which city populations
are distinguished from rural populations in underdeveloped countries.
Though little empirical research has been applied to these differences,
our factual knowledge of the non-economic impact of urbanization
is even scantier. I am aware of only one single effort which has
been undertaken by Daniel Lerner to measure in a rather rigorous way
the interrelation between urbanization and some non-economic variables (13). Lerner's primary interest was the impact of different forms
of communication upon the direction and speed of social and economic
change. His empirical work was done primarily in the Muslim
countries of the Middle East, but he later developed a series of
propositions which are applicable to all countries regardless of their
level of economic development. Lerner's reasoning begins with the
very plausible proposition that countries with different social structures and above all different educational levels of the population will
use different forms of communication. In particular, the mass media
of communication: press, radio, and movies, will be found in countries
with higher literacy levels, whereas oral communication will be found
in countries (and by implication in parts of a country) with lower literacy levels. In fact, Lerner found that literacy is very highly correlated

with daily newspaper circulation and the number of radio receivers in a community and somewhat less highly correlated with cinema seating capacity.

Lerner next proceeded to test three hypotheses which he developed on the basis of these findings, as well as other observations in the field. These three hypotheses are: I. literacy and population density, in the absence of urbanization, vary inversely and are negatively correlated; II. an increase in urbanization is associated with an increase in literacy and the use of mass communication media, regardless of the population density; III. when urbanization exceeds a certain figure, literacy and the use of mass communication media will be high, regardless of population density, but will no longer be raised by further progress of urbanization (14). These hypotheses may be combined by saying that urbanization is a necessary condition of literacy (and the use of mass media) in densely populated societies, and may be a sufficient condition of high literacy when it passes a certain point in all societies.

A test of these relationships on the basis of United Nations and UNESCO data on literacy, degree of urbanization (i.e., proportion of population in cities over 50,000 inhabitants), and density of population for seventy-three self-governing countries, yields on the whole a high degree of confirmation of Lerner's three hypotheses. Since we are here interested, above all, in the impact of urbanization upon some non-economic variables which may have relevance for economic growth, Lerner's findings on his test of the last hypothesis are of the greatest interest for us. His results are presented in Table IX-3.

This table shows rather conclusively that urbanization is an important factor in the level of literacy up to the point at which approximately one-fourth of the population lives in cities of 50,000 or more. Beyond this point literacy is only little affected by further urbanization.

Table IX-3. Degree of Urbanization and Literacy Rates in 71 Self-
            Governing Countries

Number of Countries	Literacy	Urbanization (Mean)	Population Density (per Square Kilometer)
22	over 80%	28.0%	1.293
4	61-80	29.2	6.223
10	41-60	25.0	8-111
13	21-40	17.0	6-124
22	20% and less	7.4	3-143

This table shows rather conclusively that urbanization is an important factor in the level of literacy up to the point at which approximately one-fourth of the population lives in cities of 50,000 or more. Beyond this point literacy is only little affected by further urbanization. The results of this table appear in even sharper focus if we group the various countries into three classes, those with 25 or more per cent of their population in cities of over 50,000, those with 10 to 25 per cent of their population in cities of this size, and those with less than 10 per cent of cities of this size. We then find that literacy in countries of the first class is over 50 per cent, that literacy in the last class is below a quarter of the population, and that literacy in the second, intermediate class lies between 50 and 20 per cent of population. Correspondingly the preponderant forms of communication in the first class are the mass media; in the last class, oral communication, usually in the form of commands and orders given by persons in high status positions; and in the intermediate class, mixed, comprising both some rudimentary mass media and oral communication.

Although Lerner's findings do not go beyond these correlations, we can draw some fairly obvious implications from them. Literacy is a fairly precise index for many other skills based upon it. For example, in societies with a high literacy rate we also find a larger proportion of the population in technically skilled jobs, we find better trained and larger numbers of professional persons, and better administrative, white collar, and managerial performance. Secondly, literacy is, on the whole, an important prerequisite for democratic forms of government, just as the availability

of mass media of communication -- as against communication by oral
transmission -- is an important aspect of mass participation in political
decision-making. We might pursue the implications of increased literacy
and increased employment of mass media of communication further, especially in the impact they exert on changing patterns of social values and
social behavior, and, more importantly, as has been shown by Lerner also,
on the capacity of individuals to experience empathy, i.e., to envisage and
appraise new situations outside their immediate sensual perception. It is
not necessary to insist that this heightened capacity for empathy is an important socio-psychological determinant of innovating behavior, and hence
of economic development.

Lerner's investigation is concerned only with differences in urbanization, literacy, and the use of mass media as between different countries.
For lack of more detailed data, he took averages for the various countries
of the world. However, I believe that here is a point where a conclusion
a maiori ad minus is appropriate. In other words, the differences which
prevail between countries with different degrees of urbanization may be
assumed to hold also in approximately the same degree between different
regions within one country. This is even more likely in countries with
little industrialization, since, as we have seen earlier, there are significant socio-structural differences between the countryside and the cities.
Now according to Lerner's findings, one of the crucial breaking points is a
degree of urbanization of 10 per cent. Since Lerner includes under "urban"
all places with more than 50,000 inhabitants, he uses a classification
which is somewhat different from that presented in Table IX-1 of this
paper. But we find that, with the exception of Hong Kong, Japan, Malaya,
and Korea, none of the Asian countries has more than 14 per cent of its
population in urban places of more than 20,000 inhabitants, and more than
7 per cent in metropolitan places of more than 100,000. Thus we do not go
wrong in assuming that with the exception of these four countries, all

Asian countries fall in that group of nations in which approximately not more than 10 per cent are urban as defined by Lerner. In Africa the degree of urbanization is, if anything, still lower than in Asia. In the countries of Asia and Africa, an increase in urbanization will contribute to an increase in literacy, the use of mass media of communication, and the additional consequences which follow from these developments. Yet, at the same time, we have found that in terms of distribution of the labor force, these countries are "over-urbanized," and this verdict must be further sustained in terms of the economic potential of the urban population in Asian and African countries.

A real dilemma emerges here since, on the one hand, efforts should be made in Asia to encourage rural industrialization, since urbanization has reached, for the time being, a more than optimum level, and on the other hand, further urbanization would be likely to lead to improvements in literacy and the social and economic consequences brought about by higher levels of literacy. If we assume moreover that literacy increases in the propinquity of cities and towns, the problem appears in even starker focus. One important solution of this dilemma appears to be the drafting and implementation of plans for urban or quasi-urban developments which will tend to reduce the degree of primateness in Asia. In other words, the problematical situation of Asian cities consists not merely in the average overall degree of urbanization as compared with the distribution of the labor force, but also in the absence of more viable systems of cities, i.e., of systems which correspond more precisely to a Pareto distribution (15).

V

The gradual evolution of such a system of cities demands, above all, the filling up of the gap that exists at present between the primate metropolis and the larger number of small and even minute country towns. But since these medium-sized cities and towns need an economic basis for their existence, a dispersal of secondary and tertiary occupations is one of the conditions of evolution of a system of cities.

This problem has been recognized in Asia and proposals have been made embodying various forms of dispersal of industry. One of the best known and most widely discussed proposals along this line is the strengthening of small-scale and cottage industries; others are the dispersal of even larger-scale plants over a larger number of villages and towns than has been the case before.

Both the strengthening of cottage industries and the attempts at dispersal of industrialization have still other motives behind them than avoidance of excessive growth of a few primate urban centers. They are contingent upon subsidiary developments, chiefly of transportation facilities, power sources, and marketing facilities. This fact alone points to the different problems which exist in an industrialization program concentrated in a few cities as against a widely dispersed one.

We have emphasized in the preceding discussion a series of private and social costs imposed by city life which are absent or almost absent in the country. However, these costs -- some of which are not measurable -- are presumably outweighed by benefits, which are also most difficult to measure in precise terms. Most important among these, from the viewpoint of social -- as well as private -- benefits is the fact that in cities external economies of substantial size can be made, which appear of sufficient magnitude in some cases to make all the difference as to whether certain forms of industrialization are economically feasible or not. These external economies have been discussed so often that it is not necessary to analyze them here in detail (16). In general, they consist in the availability of various subsidiary services such as

transportation and warehousing facilities, enterprises supplying information, performing marketing services, banking facilities, easy
access to efficient communication media, availability of repair and
other service agencies, for machinery and tools, and easier access
to a relatively well functioning labor market. All or most of these
facilities are absent in villages or small towns, and this may sometimes cause serious breakdowns in the operations of an industrial
enterprise or impose considerable costs upon it which it would not
have to bear if it were located in a city.

The major form of rural or small-town industrialization which
has, therefore, been proposed is the location of small-scale or handicraft industries in places outside the larger cities, and the concentration
of large-scale industry in the big cities themselves. To the extent
to which the occupational structure of cities is as yet characteristic
of pre-industrial primate cities, i.e., as long as a large proportion
of the urban population is composed of self-employed artisans,
peddlers, or of actually unemployed, further industrialization, on a
large or medium scale, is clearly called for. This development is
necessary not only in order to assure the optimum integration of the
urban economy in the process of economic development, but also in
order to forestall political developments in the cities from taking on
totalitarian or other disrupting features.

The further development of large-scale industry in cities will, of
course, not by itself eliminate the many small self-employed artisans
that are now being found there. As has been observed in the more
highly developed countries, the growth of large scale industry does not
replace small enterprises completely, but changes their form and nature.
Instead of large and small-scale firms in the same industry existing
side by side, the smaller firms tend to perform economic functions
subsidiary to the output of the larger firms: for example, the develop-

ment of a mass-production automobile industry, which is characteristically organized in plants of giant size, calls forth the development of garages, gasoline stations, repair shops, on the one hand, but also suppliers of various parts such as stoplights, windshield wipers, etc., on the other. Characteristically the producers who "cluster" around the manufacture of automobiles are small-scale enterprises.

Thus the "ideal" pattern of industrialization for Asian countries, given the present situation of "over-urbanization," the existence of actual or threatening underemployment on farms, and the desire for relatively rapid betterment of living conditions for the masses of the population would seem to call for a series of concerted measures. In the cities which already enjoy to some extent the benefits of external economies for industries of various sorts, further growth of large-scale industry should be planned. For the rest of the country, chiefly small-scale industries clustering around a few nuclei of small and middle-sized towns should be developed. The products for large-scale and small-scale industry will differ. For example, it is well known that in the Draft of the Second Five Year Plan for India, large-scale industries are prescribed primarily for heavy capital goods, whereas small-scale and cottage industry is to be developed in consumers goods industries. Such a division may be a bit too sweeping, since there are certain consumers goods which lend themselves well to large-scale production (e.g., cheap cotton textiles), and there are some capital goods which lend themselves to production on a small scale (e.g., gauges and measuring instruments).

Any such simultaneous development of large and small-scale industry and its location in large cities and smaller towns or villages faces two problems. First can small-scale industries be devised so as not to be a more temporary solution, i.e., so as to be sufficiently economical not to be pushed out of existence after a short life by gradually developing larger plants? The second problem relates to planning industrial development in such a way as to insure dispersal of industry, on the one hand, and yet not to sacrifice, in the process, locational advantages and advantages deriving from external economies. In conclusion, I shall address a few remarks to these two points.

Little needs to be said about the question of whether economical and technically efficient small-scale and cottage industries can be established, since this point has been answered affirmatively in a number of places (17). A good deal of the discussion about the role of small-scale and cottage industry in economic development has been obscured because different advocates (or adversaries) of this type of industrialization had in mind different objectives which small-scale plants were to meet. Depending upon whether cottage industries are expected to be used chiefly as a countervailing instrument against actual or threatening rural unemployment or underemployment, whether they are to be a means of attracting additional foreign exchange, or of reducing imports, different types of products and different methods, as well as different timing of development of such industries, will be desirable. Whatever may be some of the accessory purposes of support for small-scale industries, their main purpose should be to further the economic growth of the country in which they are located. Though at first considerations of make-work or saving of foreign exchange were paramount in the eyes of those who discussed small-scale and cottage industries, a new attitude is being expressed more recently. This "new look" for small-scale industry was explained by the Director General of the International Labor Organization in 1953, when he said:

> The problem will be to develop a new type of industry -- radically different both from the present cottage and handicraft industries and from the present large-scale factory industries -- which for the same amount of capital investment can at the same time pro-

duce more than the former and provide more employment than the latter. The solution of the problem of under-employment depends in large measure on the possibility of achieving this (18).

In this statement the employment argument still prevails, but in view of the different relative scarcity of productive factors in Asia and the Western world, a form of industrialization which is oriented in the direction of maximum productive employment of the human factor is at the same time also one in which scarce (and hence expensive) capital tends to be substituted by the more plentiful (and hence cheaper) labor. This opinion of the Director General of the ILO has become more and more widely accepted in Asian countries. In Burma and Indonesia, and most importantly, in India, the development of small-scale powered industry has been included in governmental development plans. The reports of the representatives of the ECAFE Study Group on Small-Scale Industry presented on the occasion of the inspection tour of Japanese small-scale industry presents further evidence for this attitude. Delegate after delegate expressed his appreciation of the Japanese achievement in creating an efficient small-scale industry and the hope that his country could do likewise (19). Perhaps the best summary of the position widely held among planners and members of industrialization commissions and similar agencies in South Asia was presented by the delegate from Ceylon. He said that the new Minister for Industries, Sir Kantiah Vaithianathan recently concluded that:

> ...the failure of previous industrialization plans is directly attributable to the fact that at the prevailing stage of industrialization in Ceylon, neither large-scale industry nor pure cottage industry (as these terms are generally understood) can be considered appropriate to solve Ceylonese economic and industrial problems. He has therefore propounded the theory (quite novel to Ceylon) that Ceylon's immediate industrial future is almost entirely in the field of small-scale industry. It is difficult to define the range of small-scale industry, but in general,

Sir Kantiah considers that the following considerations
should apply: I. the industry must be competitive and work
to commercial standards sufficient for all purposes; II. the
industry must be more labour-intensive and less capital-
intensive; III. there must be sufficient mechanization to
enable production and productivity to be competitive, but not
simply for the purpose of monopoly or control by capital or
merely to avoid trade union action; IV. the element of private enterprise must be encouraged to the maximum extent
possible (20).

This statement expresses very well the manifold dimension in which
small-scale industry may contribute to the economic development of
countries in the overall economic position of most countries in South
and East Asia. Perhaps one should add two further points to the
enumeration of the Ceylonese delegate, i.e., that small-scale industries should not be concentrated in the large primate centers, and
that the establishment of a small-scale industry should be motivated
not by the desire to introduce make-work schemes, but to contribute
to the effective economic development of the country. The more room
for the free exercise of private initiative is given in the growth of
small-scale industry, the more likely will this last objective be met.
On the other hand, it is recognized that the completely free allocation
of capital in many underdeveloped countries may have undesirable
short-run effects, since often private net gains from certain enterprises are substantially larger than the net gain of the society as a
whole (21).

Provided the proper safeguards are used, small-scale industries
of a kind and technical efficiency can be developed which will contribute
to the economic growth of an underdeveloped country, and which, at the
same time, will take up some of the actual or potential surplus of labor.
As I have implied throughout a good portion of this paper, the development of small-scale industry might also be used as a means of dispersal of industrialization and the concomitant strengthening of a more

evenly distributed system of urban places. One way of achieving
this objective is the inclusion into national development plans of
urban development plans and the simultaneous development of regional
capital budgets. A full discussion of these points would require
another paper, and hence only a sketch of these two planning devices
can be presented (22).

The inclusion of urban planning into national developmental planning
is necessary because of the prospective further growth of cities in
underdeveloped countries. Unless planned provision is made for the
development of new and expansion of present urban centers, the costs
of urbanization are likely to be vast in the long run. By urban planning
some of the effects of social disorganization which occur inevitably
in the urbanization process can be mitigated. For example, the
incidence of slums and sub-standard housing can be avoided and a
more economical use of urban space than in the absence of urban
planning can be insured. Under present conditions, urban planning is
almost completely non-existent in underdeveloped countries. In part,
this is due to the very stringent financial conditions of municipalities
in underdeveloped countries, in part, to deficiencies of public administration, especially on the local level, but in part also, to the absence of
concern for urban growth in the overall development plans which are
being prepared in underdeveloped countries (23).

Urban planning can be coupled with the development of regional capital budgets. An approximation of regional capital budgets is already
in existence in large countries like India, which are composed of topo-
graphically and economically distinct areas. But even there adequate
regional capital budgets are lacking. Since a large proportion of total
capital outlays for development are made in urban areas, regional
capital budgeting would provide a guide for the distribution of these
capital outlays, chiefly for social overhead among the different portions

of a country. If industry is to be dispersed, one must obtain some reasonably accurate knowledge of the allocation of capital for the construction of social overhead installations in the various urban regions of a country. Professor Rosenstein-Roden has argued that in many underdeveloped countries, around 70 per cent of all capital outlays are made for activities "not directly productive" (24). Most of these outlays are made in cities or the environment of cities. If this estimate is accurate -- and though we do not have precise measures, we have little reason to doubt its rough validity -- the problem of how these capital outlays are distributed among various urban centers is of paramount importance. But only a relatively detailed set of regional capital budgets can provide that information.

Finally, regional capital budgets may have the advantage of contributing to the training of more efficient administrative officers on the local level, and to combat the primateness of urban patterns in the countries of Asia. The former advantage is obvious. Since regional capital budgets require a certain dispersal of economic planning activities into the outlaying regions of a country, contacts between the more highly trained officers from the central planning staffs and regional or local administrators will become closer. We may expect the net result of this contact to be an improvement of public administration in outlying regions.

The preparation of regional capital budgets also will draw the attention of economic planners to the needs for more adequate distribution of capital outlays in places other than the capital and one or two other large cities. At the present time, most economic planning in Asian countries is done by the central governments in offices located in the capital. The capital is usually the largest city; it is a primate city. It faces staggering problems, and nothing is more natural than that the largest allocations for municipal improvements go to the capital city. The need close to one's eyes always seems greater than the even greater need far away. The preparation of regional capital budgets would, however, draw plainly the attention of economic planners to inequalities and disproportions in the distribution of capital outlays, especially those made for municipal social overhead, and would tend to provide provincial and other outlying cities with a relatively larger share of social overhead capital. This would make these outlying places more attractive for the establishment of secondary and tertiary industries and would ultimately contribute to the development of a system of urban places more in conformity with a mature economy. At the same time it would contribute, in the long run, to a more economic and "balanced" pattern of economic growth.

NOTES TO CHAPTER IX

1. See Albert J. Reiss, Jr., "Functional Specialization of Cities," in Paul K. Hatt and Albert J. Reiss, eds., Cities and Society (Glencoe, Ill., 1957), pp. 555-75.

2. Robert Redfield and Milton Singer, "The Cultural Role of Cities," Economic Development and Cultural Change, Vol. 3, No. 1 (October 1954), pp. 56-59, esp. 59.

3. See Lewis Mumford, The Culture of Cities (New York, 1938), pp. 143 ff.

4. See Max Weber, Wirtschaft und Gesellschaft (Tübingen, 1947), pp. 528 ff.

5. On primate cities in general, see Mark Jefferson, "The Law of the Primate City," Geographical Review, Vol. 29, No. 2 (April 1939), pp. 226-32; on primate cities in Asia, see Norton S. Ginsburg, "The Great City in Southeast Asia," American Journal of Sociology, Vol. 60, No. 5 (March 1955), pp. 455-62, and Rhoads Murphey, "New Capitals of Asia," Economic Development and Cultural Change, Vol. 5, No. 3 (April 1957), pp. 216-243.

6. Some evidence of this pattern of urbanization is provided in the various studies included in UNESCO, Research Center on the Social Implications of Industrialization in Southern Asia, The Social Implications of Industrialization and Urbanization (Calcutta, 1956). See especially the paper by M. B. Deshmukh, "Delhi, A Study of Floating Migration."

7. Cf. Ecafe Secretariat, "Economic Causes and Implications of Urbanization in the Recent Experience of Countries in Asia and the Far East," in Philip Hauser, ed., Urbanization in Asia and the Far East (Calcutta, 1957), p. 133.

8. For example, in a social survey of occupational distribution in the cities of Taiwan, it was found that 31.8 per cent of household heads in 1953 were self-employed, and 31.3 were laborers. If we omit domestic servants, unemployed, and non-specified occupations, we find that of the remainder 55 per cent are laborers, employees, and civil servants, and 45 per cent were employers or self-employed persons. In contrast, in Chicago, in 1940, the percentage of professional and managerial personnel and employers and self-employed was 29 per cent, and of employees and workers 71 per cent. For data on Taiwan see A. F. Raper, H. S. Chuan, and S. H. Chen, Urban and Industrial Raiwan: Crowded and Resourceful (Taipei, 1954), pp. 245-47. For data on Chicago, see Eleanor Bernert, "Changes in the Occupational Structure of the Labor Force in Chicago, Philadelphia, and the United States," in Paul Hatt and Albert J. Reiss, Reader in Urban Sociology (Glencoe, Ill., 1951), p. 327.

9. For the studies sponsored by UNESCO, see the reference in footnote 6 of this Chapter. Quite recently a most impressive report with detailed data on Poona has been published which may be regarded as constituting a model survey both from the methodological standpoint and the standpoint of completeness of coverage of relevant aspects of this problem. See N. V. Sovani, D. P. Apte, and R. G. Pendse, Poona: A Resurvey (Poona, 1956). See also Raper, Chuan, and Chen, op. cit.

10. See, for example, R. B. Textor, "The Northeastern Samlor Driver in Bangkok," UNESCO, op. cit., pp. 299 ff. and passim; see also the following articles in the same work: Deshmukh, op. cit., pp. 206 ff., esp. Table 41 on p. 211; A. F. A. Husain, "Human and Social Impact of Technological Change in East Pakistan," p. 116; and P. N. Prabhu, "Bombay, A Study on the Social Effects of Urbanization," pp. 99 ff.

11. On Bombay, see Prabhu, op. cit., pp. 72-73. On poverty in Poona, see Sovani et al., op. cit., pp. 440 ff.

12. Cf. Joseph Froomkin, "Fiscal Management of Municipalities and Economic Development," Economic Development and Cultural Change, Vol. 3, No. 4 (July 1955), pp. 309-20.

13. Cf. Daniel Lerner, "Communication Systems and Social Systems: A Statistical Exploration in History and Policy," Behavioral Sciences Vol. 2, No. 4 (October, 1957), pp. 266-75.

14. These hypotheses and the discussion in the subsequent paragraphs are all taken from Lerner's paper cited in the preceding footnote.

15. On the Pareto distribution, see Rutledge Vining, "A Description of Certain Spatial Aspects of an Economic System," Economic Development and Cultural Change, Vol. 3, No. 2 (January 1955), pp. 148 ff.

16. See, for example, United Nations, Processes and Problems of Industrialization in Underdeveloped Countries (New York, 1955), pp. 11 ff.

17. See, above all, Henry G. Aubrey, "Small Industry in Economic Development," Social Research, Vol. 18, No. 3 (September 1951), pp. 269-312, and Theodore Herman, "The Role of Cottage and Small-Scale Industries in Asian Economic Development," Economic Development and Cultural Change, Vol. 4, No. 4 (July 1956), pp. 365-70, and the literature cited at the end of both essays.

18. International Labour Organization, Report of the Director General to the ILO Asian Regional Conference, Tokyo, 1953 (Geneva, 1953), p. 40.

19. In Japan the success of small-scale industry has, indeed, been impressive. But the conditions under which small-scale industry developed and continues to be maintained in Japan may not easily be copied elsewhere. Apart from important economic assistance which Japanese small industry has received (which is described in more detail in the book by Teijiro Uyeda, The Small Industries of Japan (New York, 1938), partly from the natural conditions existing in Japan and partly through legislation affecting marketing, the supply of capital, and other aspects of small-scale production, Japanese social structure has had an important influence on the long-run evolution and growth of small-scale industry. The economic factors could be imitated in other Asian countries. The particular impetus given to small-scale industry by the Japanese social structure is a unique feature of that country which cannot be transferred elsewhere. The importance of social relations upon the mode of industrial organization in Japan is excellently brought out in a paper by John Pelzel, "The Small Industrialist in Japan," Explorations in Entrepreneurial History, Vol. 7, No. 2 (December, 1954), pp. 79-93.

20. Economic Commission for Asia and the Far East, Report of the Study Group of Small-Scale Industry Experts on Their Visit to Japan, (Tokyo, 1955), (United Nations Document E/CN.11/I & T/108), pp. 200 ff., esp. pp. 204-205.

21. An example might be the use of scarce building materials for the construction of a night club or a luxury apartment house. Clearly, an adequate system of "luxury" taxation would be a suitable means of discouraging such use of capital without interference in the market as a mechanism of resource allocations.

22. For a fuller discussion of these two points, see the forthcoming paper by Lloyd Rodwin, "National Urban Planning and Regional Capital Budgets for Developing Areas," in Regional Science Association, Papers and Proceedings, III (1957), 223-32.

23. On municipal finances in underdeveloped countries, see Froomkin, op. cit.; on public administration and possibilities of its improvements, see Frederick W. Riggs, "Public Administration: A Neglected Factor in Economic Development," in The Annals of the American Academy of Political and Social Science, 305 (May 1956), 70-80. See also Catherine Bauer, "The Pattern of Urban and Economic Development: Social Implications," Ibid., pp. 60-69.

24. P. N. Rosenstein-Rodan, "Les besoins des capitaux dans les pays sousdéveloppés," Economie Appliquée, Vol. 7, No. 1-2 (January-June 1954), pp. 82-83.

ORDER FROM:
LATIN AMERICAN BOOKS
WASHINGTON, D. C. 20016